Also by Pierre L. Nichols

How Things Were – A collection of short stories

Tapioka – Free verse poetry about
the forgotten people in society

Ancient Whisperings – Imaginative stories
of life in a prehistoric village

www.pierrelnichols.com

SECRETS

OF THE

BLUE DOOR

SECRETS

OF THE

BLUE DOOR

A TRUE STORY OF BRINGING CLOSURE

TO SEXUAL ABUSE AT A RANCH FOR BOYS

PIERRE L. NICHOLS

Secrets of the Blue Door:

A true story of bringing closure to sexual abuse at a ranch for boys

Copyright ©2017 Pierre L. Nichols

ISBN: 978-1-940769-67-7

Library of Congress Contol Number: 217903745

Publisher: Mercury HeartLink

Printed in the United States of America

Secrets of the Blue Door

DEDICATION

To all my brothers that were at the
Hacienda de los Muchachos Boys Ranch:

Alan	Floyd	Paul
Albert	Forrest	Phillip
Alex	Ivan	Randy
Alfred	Jerry	Robert
Anthony	Jessie	Raymond
Billy	Jim	Richard
Bob	Joseph	Ricky
Clarence	Juan	Rudy
Clifford	Kent	Salvador
Danny	Kevin	Sammy
David	Leonard	Spec
Doran	Leslie	Steve
Douglas	Lonnie	Tay
Doug	Luke	Tomas
Dwight	Mark	Tommy
Earnest	Matt	Vance
Eddy	Michael	Vaughn
Estelano	Pat	William

You are still remembered.

ACKNOWLEDGMENTS

If it weren't for the emotional and technical support of many of my friends and helpers across the country, this memoir would never have been completed. Among those that stayed the course and helped so much, I wish to acknowledge Sharleen Daugherty, author of *Double Doll,* for her years of friendship and sharing insight as an accomplished author herself. I also wish to especially thank Dr. Leon Podles for his help in editing and his research; important to the content of my story.

Other helpers include, Teri Matelson for her technical support (Thank you for your patience), Rev. Philip Colibraro for his spiritual guidance and help, Bonnie Buckley Maldonado and Jerry V. Howell for their love and encouragement, and of course, my special childhood friend that has stayed with me throughout my life.

FOREWORD

A generation ago, two men headed to New Mexico: one to prey on boys, the other to help them. Edward Donelan, a priest, set up his Hacienda de los Muchachos Boys Ranch for boys in distress: but he was a tyrant who made boys and staff dependent on his own whims so that he could control them and sexually abuse boys in his private room, behind his Blue Door.

Pierre Nichols arrived from Ohio as a volunteer in 1969 and dedicated himself to helping at the ranch. He stayed for years, until the conflict with Donelan led to his being fired. Then the tragic death of a little boy, led Nichols' on a personal quest as he uncovered the horrors of Donelans sexual abuse. Through the trauma of trying to help the boys and resolve the abuse by Donelan, Nichols faced challenges to his faith and well-being even to the near cost of his life. Thinking he had done all he could, he chose to make a new beginning for himself in Wyoming, where he built a new life, operating his own western art gallery. But the past wasn't far behind him when later, after moving back to New Mexico in 2004, the past resurfaces in a heart wrenching series of events that finally bring closure for the boys and himself. Nichols is a natural story teller: the reader experiences his ups and downs feeling the pain of the journey he so honesty shares.

Dr. Leon J. Podles, President, Crossland Foundation; author of *Sacrilege: Sexual Abuse in the Catholic Church.*

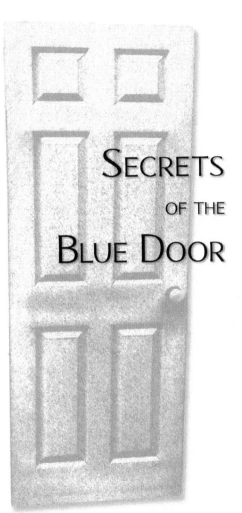

SECRETS

OF THE

BLUE DOOR

PROLOGUE

FLASHBACK

Cold grey sky fell misty upon the juniper trees. Silence, broken by raven's raucous callings, was all that dared to pierce the morning cold. I stood there, shivering as I stared into a large menacing hole carved out of the frozen ground. My glasses, smudged from hurried wipes, gave me only a shiny glimpse of children lined up along the precipice. A small-framed woman with heavy eyes of sorrow wrapped her long coat around the smallest of her two little girls. I barely recognized others standing there. Occasional blades of sunlight seemed out of place; inevitable sadness was about to intensify. The monotonous eulogy now lost in my memory. People solemnly lined up in procession like I had never seen before. The women were dressed in black, and one carried a large wooden cross.

My mind flashed with memories of my childhood. The time when Grandpa died. Grandma had met the priest at the front door with a candle and a crucifix. She slowly led him into Grandpa's bedroom. There, Father O'Connor gave Grandpa Extreme Unction, something that left Grandpa with a smile on his face. Even my own parents' burials were strangely distant experiences for me, not because of a lack of love, but because of the procedures at the cemetery. "Goodbyes" were said in the warmth of the cemetery chapel to save us from the cold winter wind. The burials were left for later – the routine work of a backhoe operator.

But there I was in the little country cemetery of Our Lady of Mount Carmel, looking down at the silvery casket, my heart crying, *Why him, why?* The procession moved closer to the fresh pile of soil. Each person took a portion of it in his hand, an offering to the dead. *What a shame,* I thought, to throw dirt on his coffin. *How could that have any meaning?* Unwillingly I followed along, bowing to the waiting soil. Cold in my hand, the grains of sand and chips of rock pressed into my skin. I squeezed as hard as I could, wanting to take away the pain of that death-soil. That caused me to reflect on a nail in the hand of one before me who loved even beyond the grave.

"Let go, just let go," I heard a woman behind me whisper. "Just let go."

EARLY YEARS 1

Nothing was more alluring than the mouthwatering aroma Grandma sent up through the stairway at breakfast time. We were happy to live above my grandparents in the West Chicago house that Grandpa Mathieu owned. We were one big family.

"Mom, can I go now? I want to go downstairs and see Grandma." I knew that she always saved one of her crepe pancakes for me.

"Finish your Wheaties, then maybe you can go, but don't be a nuisance." I gulped down the last bit of milk, followed by a quick wipe of my mouth on my sleeve, then was off to see *ma mère* with crepes on my mind. Grandpa would be sitting at the oilcloth covered table, sipping the last of his coffee from the saucer — his morning ritual.

Looking back to those days in the early 1950's, of roller skating on Haddon Avenue, of playing cowboys and Indians, I remember the patience my parents had in helping us kids to grow up. Their influence was felt like a gentle breeze, not like a wind of demands which my neighborhood friend, Johnny, had to endure. He lived across the alley from us. His father was very stern. Once his father was home from work, Johnny would always get a spanking for something he did. I remember hearing his father yelling at him just before Johnny started crying.

My father taught us with much more patience. My brother and I were told that we had to work hard if we were to get anything. Lord knows how many pails of weeds I picked and bent nails I straightened with a hammer on the sidewalk to earn my first second-hand bicycle. Mother taught us by example. Her joyful heart showed in her carefree singing around the house. Whether it was while braiding a rug, or painting with oils, or simply doing her housework, she always had a smile on her face. That was something I wanted to imitate in my life.

Above all, she gave me an awareness of an invisible friend whom I could find when we went to church. She told me that even though I couldn't see Jesus, he was nearby, my secret friend — one whom I could picture in my mind. At times, as I grew up through grade school, he was my only friend. I couldn't understand why boys made fun of me, making my books spill in the hallway and calling me names. Recess on the playground was a frightful place for me. Often I would call on my trusty friend, Jesus. He was both part reality and part imagination, together like salt and sugar in a recipe of faith.

Even with all the help I was given, I knew I was not a very good student. I drew my ABCs with the wrong hand. I had to sit in the front of the schoolroom, where Sister Regina, with her threatening ruler was watching me, should I print my words backwards. *What would become of me?*

"Wouldn't you like to be a priest, Pierre? Wouldn't that be nice, Joe?" Mom would say to Dad.

"Cubs lost again. What's that you say?"

"Never mind." Mother's ambitions for me stemmed from her cousin who was a priest in Wisconsin. Our first vacation away from home was at Father Mathieu's summer cabin on Lake Eau Claire. It was my first time seeing a priest who wasn't wearing all black. When he said mass in the cabin, Father Mathieu didn't even wear vestments. He had a motor boat and fished. I liked him. He looked like an Indian with his Mohawk haircut, dark bronze skin, and red bandana that he wore while at the lake cabin. Later, I found out that there was said to be a trickling of Native American blood in our family, from the early days in Quebec. That Indian priest was my idol at age eleven. However, I was told repeatedly by my father that to be a priest one had to know Latin. That was enough to convince me I could never be a priest. Dad was right, I wasn't smart enough. I could barely learn the Latin phrases as an altar boy, so priesthood was out.

Next came a switch from parochial school to public high school in Oak Park, Illinois. I majored in art and seriously thought about becoming an artist.

"But don't you want to be a priest, dear?"

"Oh, leave him alone, Alma. Everyone knows artists are poor and live in attics." Shot down again by my father. I began to run out of ideas. What could a boy named Pierre hope to be? *Please Jesus, don't make me a baker!*

Life went on, and I stumbled my way through high school, eventually receiving a scholarship to the Chicago Art Institute. When money ran out, I sought employment at the CB&Q railroad office building in downtown Chicago. In 1962 I decided to join the army. They let me choose: I could have a typewriter or a rifle or a camera in my hands. I was quick to choose the camera. After signal school training, I was an official Combat Still Photographer. When my orders came through for assignment, I was baffled.

"Where in the world is Thailand, Ken?" I asked my classmate.

"Hell if I know. I'm going there too. Guess we'll find out," he replied. I'll never forget stepping off the plane at the Don Mueng Airport in Bangkok. We were wearing our wool Class A uniforms. The dense humidity, heat, and aromas of Asia hit me like a wet towel in the face. That was the only time we wore Class A uniforms until our date of departure, thirteen months later.

Our assignment was with the 809th Engineer Battalion, east of Bangkok, out in the rice fields. They were constructing a major road toward the Cambodian border. Our job was to photo record the progress. It was a fairly easy assignment. About every two months, Ken and I could get R&R time. A three-day pass, with a deuce-and-a-half truck and we were on our way to the coastal village of Pattaya where the battalion rented a beach house. At that time, Pattaya was not much more than a dirt road with local houses and fishing boats. It had few, if any, motor vehicles and no commercialization.

The beach house was an airy two-story concrete building. Sleeping rooms were upstairs, with the kitchen and main room below. The first time I went there, I was somewhat perplexed by the bathroom: no toilet fixture, only a six-inch hole in the middle of the concrete floor. The main event for us was water skiing out to the islands. It was a thrill to see fish leaping and dolphins following alongside as we skied.

Later in the day, the local men would gather in a circle in the dusty street. Little children played and chased each other between their fathers, who were squatting comfortably on the ground. Soon tempers flew along with feathers, as the old men gambled over the evening cock fights. It was easy to tell which of the local men were the owners of the fighting cocks. They had gold-capped teeth and took pride showing them off to us with their wide, exaggerated smiles. Pattaya was always a nice escape from the army camp.

Another adventure we had was north of our army camp to the town of Prachinburi. We could hitch a ride there on Thai gravel trucks. Sitting on top of the gravel was the safest place to ride. Numerous such trucks had crashed when crossing the rickety bridges, so it was smart to sit on the edge, ready to jump if necessary. The reason to go to Prachinburi was to visit a Thai Catholic priest we had met once when we were there with the medic team, spraying against bubonic plaque. Father Luthep told me that my name, Pierre, was also his name in Thai. We felt that connected us.

One time there was another priest at Prachinburi with Father Luthep. He was an American missionary, Father Brennan, a priest whom I admired for his faith and mission in life. He cared for a leper colony further north near the border with Laos. Ken, who had also come with me to Thailand as a photographer, wasn't too interested in him, but another of our buddies, David, was. David and I became very interested in hearing everything about Father Brennan's mission. After several visits with Father, I began to sense a direction for my life.

Something about this soft-spoken man spoke to me. My childhood fantasies of being a missionary priest and working in some remote jungle came back as I listened to him talking about his leper colony. While Kennedy's Peace Corp was inspiring many to get out in the world to help others, I was inspired by this priest to think about what I could do.

During one of our visits I mentioned my background in art to Father Brennan. He was quick to say, "Why don't you come and help me by starting a ceramic shop at the colony, so we can make a little money for our needs." His suggestion caught me off guard — to think that he would have enough confidence in me to ask such a serious question. I started thinking seriously about how this idea would radically change my life. I had to weigh my options and try to discern the answer to my prayers. The next time we met, I was ready to give an answer. As I had hoped, Father Brennan asked me again about helping him at the leper colony. I was excited to say yes, I would return to Thailand after my military service was over. I felt confident that I could set up a small ceramic cottage industry and teach others how to work in clay. It was an exciting plan, one that I embraced, feeling that it was something God wanted me to do.

Time passed quickly during the next two years. Fort Benning, Georgia, was my last assignment, photo shooting with the airborne and ranger training programs. By 1965, I was out of the service and eager to start my adventure with Father Brennan in Thailand. He was about to return to the Chicago area to solicit funds for his leper colony. I was ready to show him drawings and plans for the ceramic project. I was ready to leave everything behind and return to Thailand, once Father gave me the OK. I felt I could do a good job at the mission; after all, Jesus would be there with me.

My mother was proud of my endeavor. In spite of failing

health, she planned to dress up for the occasion to meet Father Brennan. This was going to be the time I would know for sure God's intentions for me. We would work out the details. But my mother went into emergency surgery the same day we were to meet Father Brennan. The outcome was bleak. The message was clear. The meeting with Father was cancelled; I knew I would remain at home, helping to care for my mother. I felt let down. I thought helping Father Brennan with my ceramic project would have been perfect for me. I believed I could do it, but God was planning something different. I felt discouraged.

After the passing of my mother in February of 1967, I decided to move away from Oak Park, Illinois. I got a job as a commercial photographer in Youngstown, Ohio, close to where my sister lived. There I pursued my independent life and career. By 1969, I had acquired property at a private lake and enjoyed my sailboat on weekends. I felt that I was doing what I was meant to do. Jesus didn't need me. Then, out of the clear blue sky, I got a phone call from my army buddy, David.

"Well, how have you been, Pierre?" he shouted into the phone. Continuing at a non-stop pace, he said, "I'm going down to New Mexico for a month. This mission group I'm working with here in St. Louis wants me to go help do some carpentry work for a priest named Father Ed, who is starting a boys' ranch. Why not come on down too? We can finally be on a mission project together." His words were a painful tease, after my disappointments about Thailand and the leper colony. Several months ago, I would have said OK, but now, with my life in order, I wondered whether I should even listen to David.

"Ah, let me think about this. I'll call you back tomorrow."

There he was with another one of his wild ideas. I remembered one incident in Thailand. Our military camp was close to the river village of Phanom, a small gathering of about two dozen thatched-roofed houses on stilts. At the outskirts of the village stood the largest building of all. Its bamboo façade boasted electric flashing red lights in a universal code, welcoming all to the whore house. Late one evening, David came back to camp from Phanom all excited saying, "Three of the girls just got thrown in jail. If we go and marry them tomorrow, they can get out."

"Are you kidding?" was my edited response. Not exactly my idea of mission work. David finally calmed down and slept off his ambitious plan. The next day, David, Ken and I were all glad to remain single. Crazy as it sounded, I did admire him for his compassion, even if it was misdirected.

This time David was calling to see whether I would go to New Mexico for two weeks as a volunteer. I thought about my job, my new independence, my sailboat. I was getting to like my life. Was God messing with me? Was He testing me to see if I meant what I had said before, *whatever you want?* That night, I dusted off my old friendship with Jesus. His guidance left me in a peaceful sleep.

"Good morning, David. It's me. Thought about it last night. Kind of crazy, but you know what?" I said. "I'll do it! Let's do this mission thing together. I'll go for two weeks, just to see what it's all about. I wouldn't mind taking a break from work. Might be nice to meet a priest who is helping out kids. Send me the contact information, and I'll see you when I get there."

"Oh, by the way, Pierre. Remember that priest Father Luthep that we knew in Thailand? They made him a bishop!"

"Wow, David. I sure hope that helps me at the pearly gates. We promised each other that we would meet again in heaven. I've never forgotten that." The next day, I was granted a three-week vacation time, and a few days later I was on my way to New Mexico. I felt that I had stepped onto shaky ground, but still I felt good about what I was doing. *Thank you, Jesus, but please, make it work this time?*

THE CHALLENGE 2

"Don't burn your bridges behind you." Sitting there, coach class, window seat, I realized that that was what I might be doing. My boss at the photo agency in Youngstown sensed my excitement and didn't like the thought of me possibly leaving the company. I knew he was prepping me for a better position, but I felt that something greater was ahead for me to do, something more than just staying in a groove.

My father, who grew up in Chicago, was now living in Tucson, Arizona. When I told him of my plan to see about volunteer work in New Mexico, he was disappointed in me, offering no encouragement. "You have a good job. Why do you want to risk throwing it all away? For what?" he exclaimed. "You don't belong in New Mexico. You want to be a Mexican, do you? You're wasting your life being a volunteer in the middle of nowhere, all by yourself. You don't even know what you're going to do there."

I had no facts with which to defend myself; I didn't know much about the boys' ranch or the priest in charge of it. From David's phone call, back in Ohio — about joining him at the ranch — I got the impression that this ranch project was out in the Wild West. Would it be in the mountains or in the canyons? Would there be horses or even cattle? I could hardly wait to see David again and work together at the ranch. I felt a calling from my secret Jesus whom I had kept with me from my earliest days. Also, it sounded like a fun adventure; I had never been to New

Mexico. *It's only for two weeks!* Staring out the portal window at the wing of the passenger jet, I chuckled to myself thinking, *indeed I am going to New Mexico on a wing and a prayer!*

"Have you ever flown before?" the woman sitting next to me asked. I guess it was obvious I was hogging the window, like a child flying for the first time.

"Oh yes. This time I'm on my way to New Mexico."

"You must have family there. Do you?"

I was about to start explaining my adventure, when the stewardess asked, "Would you care for something to drink?"

"Thank you." After a quick sip, I began with my story. By the time we landed in Denver, I had babbled on for over half of an hour. Patiently, she listened, offering a smile and an occasional "Oh my!" to my story. It was encouraging to hear her approval, even though her eyes conveyed something else.

After two planes and a long bus ride, I stepped off the bus with suitcase and guitar in hand onto the empty street in Springer, New Mexico, directly in front of the Stockmen's Café. As the bus pulled away in a cloud of black exhaust, I found myself feeling totally naked before the staring eyes of two old men who were seated on a board bench several feet away. I moved over to the wall away from them, set my bag and guitar down, and leaned against the brick building in the shade.

If I looked interesting to them, so, too, did they to me. Both were characters from an Old West movie, complete with weathered Western hats, worn boots and a need to spit something in a can. The man closest to me looked the older of the two. His wrinkled face reminded me of the dried apple heads my mother carved for the character dolls which she made years ago. His dirty tan Western hat showed years of use, with its dark oily sweatband and wavy brim — perhaps a symbol of pride for his life as a cattle rancher who was now reduced to storytelling on an equally old sidewalk bench. His companion, from what I could see of him, had a full white beard and looked like Santa Claus hiding out in Small Town, New Mexico. His bib overalls, stretched tight around his plump body, fell short above grey snakeskin boots. Perhaps they too were his symbols of success. Both of the men seemed pleased to be together, sharing the afternoon event of which I was sure that I had become the main attraction.

"There's only that one bus each day, young feller. Are you waiting for someone?" the man closer to me on the bench asked.

Before I could reply, the other man tipped his hat back on his head and said to his friend, "See there Harold. He got him a fiddle case. Why he's gonna play at the Cactus Bar tonight. Won't that be just fine?"

"Don't pay no mind to John. He don't always hear things right in his head," Harold said to me, revolving his finger next to his ear.

"Well," I said, "I'm here, waiting for a friend, a Mr. Garcia, to pick me up from the ranch."

"Which Garcia you look'n fer? We have a lot of them around here," Harold asked with a chuckle.

"Do yah sing too?" John joined in.

"No, John, he's going to a ranch!" Harold shouted back.

"With a fiddle?" John again asked, with signs of confusion on his face.

I was saved by a van pulling up at the curb. The driver got out and walked around the back to meet me. "Hello," he said to me with his hand extended. "You must be Pierre. My name is Tony Garcia from the boys' ranch. Welcome to New Mexico." *Thank God for the rescue.*

"You gentlemen have a nice day now," I said to the twosome on the bench. Mr. Garcia put my belongings in the back of the van and I climbed in. Away we went, headed out of town.

Mr. Garcia was the Assistant Director of the Hacienda de los Muchachos Boys Ranch. He was a short Hispanic man in his late thirties, with a pleasant smile and friendly voice. He told me that he came along with Father Ed from where they had both worked at the New Mexico Boys' Correctional Facility, located on the west side of Springer, New Mexico. The then-Archbishop of Santa Fe, Edwin Byrne, had given Father Ed the OK to be Chaplain there. After deciding that he wanted to start his own boys' ranch, Father Ed with Mr. Garcia, left to start the Hacienda de los Muchachos, just months before my arrival.

Our talk on the thirty-five-mile drive East to the boys' ranch was pleasant; however, my eyes took complete precedence over my ears as I stared out the side window at the passing prairie. Dry rusty grass stretched like a carpet cut straight at the horizon's edge. Occasional spots were tiny structures in the distance, looking like toys abandoned for a better game. The magnetic beauty of earth and sky pulled me, as if calling to me to belong. I surrendered. I was mesmerized.

Now I was at last going to see this ranch and meet the priest,

Father Ed Donelan, who started the boys' ranch. "We're almost there," Mr. Garcia said as we rounded the corner off Highway 56. "Oh, by the way," he added with a smile, "Just call me Tony." That was for me a welcome sign of acceptance.

About two miles ahead, in the middle of the empty prairie, I could see an island of sparse trees with a few structures clustered among them. *Is that the ranch?* I thought. As we got closer I saw that the island was a gathering of left-over houses from what use to be a small town. The closest thing to a town center was a closed-up mercantile building on the right and a flat-roofed stucco building on the left. Perhaps it had been a small motel back in some better time. Other than these two buildings, there were no signs of any businesses or even people. Two tan short-haired dogs lay comfortably in the gravel, caring little about our arrival as we passed by. After that, all there was to see of the place, was an empty looking house surrounded by, treeless lots marked by sagging wire fences, an occasional clothesline pole and worn down concrete foundations — grave markers for houses long gone. The whole area of this one-time-town couldn't have been much more than eight blocks. Straight ahead of us a cattle guard marked the town border. Beyond that, the empty prairie rolled its way north into distant hills and extinct volcanic cones. It was a peaceful however lonely looking view; perhaps a premonition of my life to come.

"This town use to be at the end of a railroad line out of Clayton to the east," Tony explained. "Never did make it to Springer. Grew lots of beans around here though. Right before the war, they sold off all the steel rails to the Japs. Most people had their houses moved elsewhere. Not much left now." As Tony turned right down a gravel street, I was about to ask him what the big old building in front of us was, when he said, "Here's the ranch."

Oh, my God! What am I getting myself into? This "ranch," this "Hacienda de los Muchachos Boys Ranch," was a large sprawling adobe building, the onetime district high school at the edge of town. Tony told me that it had been phased out and closed several years ago. Just four months ago, Father Ed had signed the lease on the building to start the ranch. It was a huge structure and looked like a battleship among scattered rowboats. *Try not to look discouraged.*

Tony drove the van into the property and stopped in front of the main entrance of the large stucco building. There, outside of the building at the top of the flagstone steps, stood Father Ed. He looked like a giant!

For some reason, I had imagined him in black with a Roman collar, looking like the priests I had seen before. But my eyes found nothing familiar to make me feel comfortable. Instead, I scanned quickly over this tall person of fifty-something years. Wearing no hat, his grey-white full head of hair, with his unshaven beard, framed a face that told of both pride and authority. His overweight burly physique bulged under a simple short-sleeved tee shirt. Held up by a black leather belt, his black pants fell long and straight until crumpling atop dusty black engineer boots. Obviously, he was a man of his own design. Mr. Garcia had told me that Archbishop Davis, who replaced Edwin Byrne, gave Father Ed permission to start the boys' ranch, but without any diocesan funding, so Father Ed was on his own doing things his own way.

My train of thought was broken by Tony's saying, "OK,

Pierre, time to get out of the van." It was a short walk to the porch, but enough time for me to mumble a quick prayer.

"Hi, Father," I said, as I introduced myself. He grasped my hand tightly and pulled me into his six-foot-five-inch-tall self. The crushing embrace was an embarrassing bear hug. I felt repulsed by his sweaty, smelly tee shirt and I was intimidated by him, as, I supposed, others also were.

"Welcome, Pierre, to my boys' ranch," he said. He opened wide the double glass entrance doors for me.

As we walked into the large main lobby of the building, the coolness of the adobe structure was a welcome relief from the summer heat. The concrete floor and tall plastered walls made me feel as if I was in a cave, or perhaps in an impressive public building. From the lobby, Father ushered me into the nearby dining room; dry, thirsty floor boards creaked with every step we took. This was a sound that would become familiar to me over the coming years.

We sat at a large, round, nicely-covered table and talked over iced tea while a window fan hummed, blowing hot air into the dining room. To the right of the table, I noticed a half-closed Dutch door. From within that next room I could hear utensils and pans being moved about. Seeing that I was distracted by the kitchen noise, Father Ed said, "Mrs. Garcia is our cook until we get a fulltime cook for the ranch."

"Oh, that's nice." I replied, trying to show Father that I was giving him my full attention. He continued to explain what he expected of his staff, such as: no smoking, no drinking and no use of the ranch vehicles for private use. I felt pleased with myself; I thought that I had passed the first round of qualifications.

When the moment seemed right, I asked Father Ed where David was since I was eager to see him again. Until now, Father seemed to be easy going and mild mannered. When I asked him about David, his whole demeanor changed. He clenched his mouth, and through tightly-held teeth replied, "David had to leave early!" Very slowly he lowered his glass to the table to emphasize his control over the situation. I was dumbfounded by his angry reply. *What had happened?*

Judging by the stern look on his face, I decided that it wasn't the time to be asking any more questions about David. Then, just like the switching of a lamp from dark to light, he returned to his calm self and said, "Let me show you the building, Pierre. As you will see, it isn't in very good condition, but it's a start." I got up and followed him back into the main lobby, glad to be on my feet and away from an uncomfortable situation.

The entrance lobby, I was told, was where Father would hold daily general meetings with the staff and the boys. It was lined on both sides with chairs of various shapes and sizes. At both ends of the lobby were steel double doors. Walking toward the south end of the hall, Father said, "These steel double doors separate the south wing of the building. The old school rooms are now the boys' dorm rooms. Staff are NOT allowed behind these doors without my permission." Again, I got his stern look as if he was making sure I understood the importance of what he had just said — and I did.

The open doors revealed a long, mostly dark hallway with concrete floor, tall walls, and more double doors at the far end. The frosted glass window panes in those doors were the only source of light in the hallway, other than some light coming from the side rooms and cutting across the hall floor. As we walked down the hall, Father pointed out the room that was for the younger boys, as well as those for the older boys. By now it was afternoon and the boys who were not at school in Springer were taking their daily siesta. As we passed by one room, I got a quick peek inside and noticed a partition wall of two-by-fours, waiting to be finished with wallboard. Perhaps this was a project David left unfinished. The condition of the rooms was dismal. The large windows were weathered and partly covered with poorly fitting drapes. Overhead, the ceiling showed signs of serious rain damage, which left long streaks of adobe stain down the wall in one of the rooms. I felt sorry for Father Ed, with only this old building to start his ranch project, but it encouraged me as I thought of all the ways I could help.

"This room next to mine," Father said, "is for the new boys, and for any boy who has lost his privileges." *That's a strange combination.* Next came the washroom/bathroom. I was struck that this big, dimly-lit room was painted dark blue. It had only two toilets which sat exposed in a corner along the sink wall. There were no privacy dividers between them. In an equally exposed area was a single shower head and two wringer washing machines. *This building needs a lot of work!* Across from the washroom were Father's private quarters. His was the only room in the entire hall that had a door on it. That door was painted blue. There was a small sign taped to it that read, "Knock before entering." *Who would ever be entering besides Father?* I wondered.

Back through the double doors into the lobby, we took a right turn and headed toward the gymnasium. I expected to see an open floor for games. It was an impressively large gym, but more than half of the area was packed full with every kind of used appliance you could imagine. Father had been accepting donations for the ranch. These mostly useless pieces of worn-out furniture and equipment didn't impress me.

Back again, through the lobby, we went through the other steel double doors that closed off the north wing. Another long dark hall. The first room of the left had been turned into a modest chapel. The other three rooms, further down the hall, were still the original classrooms. On the right side of the long hall, all the rooms had been sealed off and converted into an apartment for Tony, his wife, and their five children.

After this quick tour of the building, we returned to the lobby to await both the end of the afternoon siesta and the arrival of the school bus from town. It was pleasant sitting in the lobby and looking out the glass front doors. The afternoon sun shining in through the doors seemed to soften the concrete floor. I was beginning to relax and I had a good feeling that this was going to be a great adventure. *Thank you, Jesus.* That was what I wrote in the first of my little diaries that I kept over the years.

No sooner than we had sat down, Father got up, pulled his large rotund frame into a standing position, and disappeared behind the steel double doors. I heard him singing in a loud echoing voice, "God is love, and he who abides in love abides in God, and God in him." That, I learned, was his way of letting the boys in their rooms know that it was time to get up from their siesta.

Within minutes, out came ten sleepy-eyed boys in shorts and tee shirts and some odd foot wear. Father explained that he always took a new boy to Raton on a buying trip. He would take them to Solano's Boots & Western Ware Store and outfit each with new clothes. One of the boys gleamed with pride as he passed me and showed off his new boots. Obviously, he was a new arrival. With the last boys, out of the dorms, Father returned to the lobby, closed the double doors behind him, and assumed his place of authority — sitting directly in front of the glass front doors. He motioned for me to come sit in the chair next to him.

The stage was set as we waited for the school bus to arrive from Springer with the rest of the boys. All I could do was try to act casual, while the boys, seated in the entrance hall, looked me over. As I looked around the hall at the boys, I couldn't help smiling at them. They reminded me of my own youth as a Boy Scout, when we were youngsters, laughing and teasing, goofing around as kids. These boys seemed the same to me. I didn't see problem boys, just kids needing activities to absorb their energy. I felt confident that I could get them involved with the outdoors.

An obvious mini-fight was going on over who was going to sit next to me. A stern look from The Boss, Father Ed, settled the issue. No one was allowed to sit next to me. Moments later the school bus pulled up in front of the school . . . I mean, ranch house. I sensed that the school bus was the only connection between the outside world and the world of Father Ed's ranch.

In filed five tired-looking older boys, each silently taking his seat along the hall; I assumed that this was standard procedure for a school day. With everyone in place, the afternoon meeting began. Father broke the silence saying, "Pierre is here from Ohio and will be visiting for two weeks." With no more explanation, he turned his attention to the list of chores and indicated which boys were assigned to them. Whether it was the morning, noon, or evening meeting, I saw a pattern emerge as days went by. Boys got jobs such as kitchen helper, laundry, rabbits, outdoor chores, etc., mostly based on how Father liked them. Sometimes one or two boys seemed to be especially favored. Father Ed was stern in running the ranch. I saw clearly that the boys needed someone to involve them in activities. I saw my place at the ranch, a place where I could be useful. What would happen in the next two weeks? Would I be accepted as a potential staff member willing to work to the drum beat of Father Ed, or could I become a big brother or a friend to the boys? But, I reminded myself, I was only going to be there for two weeks. *Slow down, Pierre. You have the cart in front of the horse!*

Getting to know the boys was a slow process. They seemed anxious to know me as well as to see how I was getting along with Father Ed. I was happy to take a few boys for short hikes and I enjoyed spending time with them outside. In the evening, Father Ed and I discussed ranch plans and how I could be more involved, should I decide to return as a full-time volunteer. As the two weeks were ending, I felt there was a place for me at the ranch. I knew it would be a complete change of lifestyle, as well as a real commitment to leaving behind my desires for success. I prayed over it and felt I had the correct answer to give Father Ed when the time would come.

That time came, and once again we were at the dining room table, the night before Tony was to drive me to Springer, on my way back to Ohio. I knew I wanted to return to the ranch. In my heart, I knew it. That very morning when I was out behind the building walking with a few of the boys, one of them stopped me and said, "You won't return. No one does." That comment hit me like a brick. He looked deeply disappointed, because he believed what he had said to me. I thought I was going to be making a commitment to Father Ed, but at that moment in front of me stood the one person, the one little boy to whom I was really going to make my commitment. The moment of truth. I smiled back at him as I put my hand on his shoulder and said, "Maybe I'm different? Come on, Rudy. Let's go look at the hogs."

Sitting before Father Ed, I felt confident as I gave him my answer. "I would like to return to help as a volunteer, and I will make a commitment for a full year." He seemed genuinely pleased. His smile of acceptance made me feel good. God had brought us together for a purpose. What it would all be, I wasn't too sure. All I could think was, *stay with me, Jesus!*

The flight back to Ohio and the following weeks went painfully slow as I hurried about closing out my job and getting things in order. Keeping in mind my commitment to the boys made it easier when it came time to sell my sailboat. After that, the antiques went and what was left I put in storage. It made me feel empty, like a blank canvas waiting for a new "me" to be painted on it.

No one seemed to approve of my decision, but I continued to believe in my mission. I was pleased, thinking that now I could be doing things that would help others. I had hopes of getting in contact with David once I was back in Ohio, but all my efforts to locate him failed. I couldn't find the right missionary center in St. Louis, or an address in Chicago, where he was from. I could only hope he was well and that perhaps we would meet again.

This time, rather than flying back to New Mexico, I drove my jeep, packed with what I thought I needed in my new life out West. I was excited. I could hardly wait to get back and see the ranch and everybody, especially the look on little Rudy's face when he saw me returning.

THE ADVENTURE BEGINS 3

I was happy and comfortable to be back at the boys' ranch. I had no doubt it would be a challenge to work with Father Ed. I could tell he was set in his ways; I would have to accept that. The day I arrived at the ranch, Mrs. Garcia had baked a large sheet cake to welcome me back. That evening, Father announced that I was now, an official volunteer staff member. The boys were excited: cake!

The volunteer Knights of Columbus men from Los Alamos, New Mexico, were helping out by constructing several small staff apartments in front of the main ranch building. With one of them completed, it was offered to me along with a monthly stipend of twenty-five dollars and my own trip to Solano's for boots. It was a nice little apartment and like the rest of the ranch, I had no phone, TV or radio, but it didn't matter to me. I would have plenty else to do, helping Father Ed and the boys.

Very soon, I became involved in teaching evening classes. I was allocated the last room on the left down the north hall. This became my classroom for drawing and art. I also became ranch photographer and took hundreds of slides of daily life at the ranch. This also gave me the opportunity to teach the boys something about photography.

Within several months, Father and I went on a buying trip to Albuquerque where he purchased a ceramic kiln and supplies for my clay class. The mysterious ways of God. He knew, better than I, when and where I would be teaching ceramics: not in Thailand at a leper colony, but here at a boys' ranch in New Mexico. That realization empowered me. I would spend up to eighty hours a week working on class projects, architectural drawings for the proposed new ranch buildings, managing the boy's laundry and outdoor chores with the boys. This last assignment included helping the boys with everything from watering the old elm trees that lined the front of the building, to feeding and caring for the hogs, one horse and the rabbits.

Aside from chores and after-hours class prep work, I enjoyed taking some of the boys down to the creek for a hike in the afternoon. Another activity I could do with the boys was taking one or two for short night walks to study the stars. Once it was dark enough we would leave the ranch building and walk down the empty blacktop road north of town — never too far away, just far enough so we could feel distant from everyone else. There was no chance of vehicles, so we would lie down on the warm pavement and stare up at the heavens. Sometimes we would make up ghost stories or just let our minds wander.

On one of those warm summer nights I had Jessie and Ivan with me. Jessie, a real talker, was the younger of the boys, while Ivan was usually the quieter of the two. We were lying on our backs looking up at the stars and the Milky Way. Ivan broke the silence asking, "Where does rain come from?" The question didn't seem to fit the moment, but I gave him the best answer I could. I said, "Ivan, storm clouds are like steam in a pot of hot soup. That steam turns into drops of water on the inside of the lid. The storm clouds," I continued, "are steam, and cold air is the invisible lid in the sky. When the clouds hit the cold air, they turn into drops of water and fall."

"Rain!" shouted Ivan as he raised his arms, sweeping the night sky with fingers of delight. I was proud of him and of myself for coming up with a good answer. After a while, confident at answering anything, I asked them both, "Where do you think all those stars come from?" I was ready to give them a very impressive mini lecture on astronomy.

Before I had a chance though, Ivan blurted out, "They are diamonds from the hand of God, and my Mom said that there's one diamond up there for each person in heaven."

Jessie sat straight up when he heard that. With eyes glued to the night sky as if searching for something, he said, "Then there's one up there for my father. He got shot dead running from the liquor store."

Silence fell upon us until I finally said, "You know something. Both of you are right." *Thank you, God, for your guidance.* What a night. I remember it well.

During my first year at the ranch, I was the only volunteer staff member, not counting Mrs. Garcia who helped out in the kitchen. Soon Father hired a full-time cook named Irene. She was a single, middle-aged woman, rather quiet, who kept to herself. She lived in an old trailer behind the gymnasium, one that Father Ed had moved from Springer for her use. She stayed the longest of all the cooks. Irene was dedicated to helping the boys in the kitchen. She was always sensitive to not showing too much affection toward a boy, so that Father Ed wouldn't get jealous and reassign him out of the kitchen. Frankie was one of her favorites. Since he had some learning disabilities, he had trouble doing two tasks in a row. Irene patiently drew pictures for him, showing step by step how to prepare foods. She gave each boy a sense of her motherly love, helping boys like Frankie more than Father Ed ever knew about.

Sometime during the second year of my commitment as a volunteer, Father was able to get two Catholic nuns from Boston to come and help at the ranch. They were housed in another used trailer that was out back near Irene's trailer. One of the nuns, who was in fact Father's older sibling, was named Sister Sarah. She was the epitome of "nunhood." When she first got to the ranch, she insisted on wearing her shiny patent leather shoes; she sat prim and proper in her designated hall chair at meetings, silent as if in prayer. Sister Sarah, bless her heart, did a good job teaching music even though she was tone deaf. Every boy had to learn to play the recorder. Versions of "Mary had a Little Lamb" echoed through the long halls every afternoon, second only to Father Ed's, "God is love…"

Sister Mary Carmel was the other nun. She was younger and a bit flamboyant with her red skirt and flowery apron, something she would never have worn back at the Mother House in Boston. She kept busy with teaching reading classes for the boys who couldn't go to school in town. Sister also took on the job of organizing clothing donations which were kept in a separate room down the hall from the chapel. Once the Sisters were around the boys, their routines changed. Both still kept their religious head piece and shoulder length veil; however, the polished shoes and proper English all went out the window. They became "countryfied" and loved it!

The Hacienda de los Muchachos Boys Ranch was known around

the state as a place where the courts, as well as parents, could send their boys for needed guidance, guidance that was assured by a Catholic priest. Income for the ranch came from donations, which were mainly generated by Father's mailing list and his famous begging trips. He would take a few select boys in the new blue van and go to a New Mexico town. There he would get a motel with the boys and give begging talks at the local Catholic church. Of course, the older boys secretly competed to win favor with Father so they would be picked to go on his next begging trip. Father had quite a following around the state. He was known as "The Juvenile's Beggar," who begged for the sake of his boys. I was pleased to help, however I could, when he was away.

Often it gave me the chance to spend more time with the boys who were left behind at the ranch. Sometimes we would sit around and sing as I played the guitar. Since the boys were not allowed to have a radio or TV in their dorm rooms, my guitar became the only source of music, the only one, that is, other than the recorders. The boys liked making up songs with me.

Don't think these boys weren't tough. I was twenty-seven when I started at the ranch in 1969, and they really gave me a workout. I would take the old ranch van that we called the Giddy-Up Bus, full of as many boys as I could fit in it, down to Ute Creek. There we would play all kinds of physically exhausting games.

In the summer, when it was hot, there was swimming at our favorite swimming hole. Other times there was gang-up style Hide-and-go-Seek. That was a version mothers might not have approved. The boys all loved the idea of running away, hiding somewhere around the rocks and shrubs, and eventually being discovered. Looking back at those times, I think that the best feeling they got out of it was that of being found. Sometimes it took hours before the gang found the last one's hiding place.

In the deep of winter, when the coldest weather froze the shallow creek thick with six-inch ice, the boys loved the crazy challenge to see who was going to be first to hop across the floating sheets of ice without falling in. I admit it was one of my coolest ideas...no pun intended. All the boys got to be challenged and to revel in their success. The game was over when we were all wet, laughing our way home to the warm Hacienda. They kept me on my toes. All those crazy ideas and challenges — ice hopping, rock climbing and critter-catching stunts — I had to do them first!

Not all my experiences with the boys were pleasant. Some of the boys didn't care for me, and some of them I wasn't able to connect with. Often, I wished I could know something of their past so I could have some pointers on how to help them. Father Ed refused to share anything about from where or how a boy got to the ranch or indeed anything about their pasts. It was obvious, as time went by, that Father Ed tried to drive a wedge between the boys and anyone, even a boy's parents, who tried to befriend the boys. He would not allow any parents to visit the ranch or to be in contact with their child. He made sure each boy knew that Father Ed was their only parent, their only father.

This was the case one Christmas evening. Christmas Day for the ranch involved a traditional trip in the vans. Father Ed, the staff, and the boys would all get in both vans and go singing Christmas songs at the hospitals and nursing homes in Springer,

Raton and Clayton. It was a very long day, but everyone enjoyed giving joy to others. Back at the Hacienda, Mrs. Garcia, who helped in the kitchen, would have a full festive Christmas dinner ready for everyone.

After dinner came the big event of gift giving. Of course, the only one allowed to give out gifts was Father Ed. On one Christmas evening, Father Ed showed his jealousy of parents in a cruel way. He announced in front of everyone that he had sent back numerous gifts mailed to the boys for Christmas, saying, "If parents can't send money to support the ranch, then they shouldn't send gifts for their boy." This gave me another insight into how he made sure the boys had only one parent to answer to, that is, himself. I remember sharing in the embarrassment felt by all, since I was the only staff member that didn't get a gift from him. It was a public warning for me to not infringe on his role as father to the boys.

Occasionally, a boy might open up to me. Having them in my clay class provided such an opportunity. Clay seemed to be very therapeutic as well as revealing. Sometimes a boy would make a perfect little bowl, and other times a boy would torture and smash the clay into crumbs.

Luke was one of my best clay class students, though he didn't start out that way. He was seventeen years old, muscular, mean-looking and street-smart. He scared the wits out of the other boys. The Sisters were afraid of him because of the fiery look in his eyes. Even Father Ed seemed to leave him alone. I decided to get him involved in my clay class. At first, he didn't want to even touch the clay. It took him weeks of self-control before he could keep from squeezing the life out of it. It spoke of some deep problems he had. I would patiently say to him, "It's OK, Luke, there's still a lot of clay left."

In the winter when it was dark outside, I would have to walk down the un-lit north hallway to my evening clay classroom. I would open the double doors to the long hallway, step in, closing the doors behind me. Since it was all dark, I would find my way down the hall by running my left hand along the left wall until I came to the clay classroom door. Once there, I would open the door, then in the light of the room, turn and enter. It was my blind routine that I had pretty well memorized.

One evening, unknown to me, Luke was standing in the dark outside the classroom door waiting to ambush me. When I walked down the hall and turned the knob allowing a sliver of light to escape from the room, it hit like fire on the pale, waxy face of Luke. He was staring into my eyes, at less than five inches from my face! No sound or movement; with almost a look of hate. The moment passed so quickly I had no time to think of any consequence; a fight or even a knife to my chest. With only the breath in my mouth, I said, with a slight smile of acknowledgement, "Hello, Luke." Then I opened the door and went into the classroom as if nothing had happened. Amazingly, I never flinched or felt threatened. That evening I thought about his planned ambush. Perhaps it was his way of testing my steel; my ability to hold my own against his own persona. *How was I able to react so calmly?* I wondered. All I could conclude was that it was the peacefulness that I had in giving of myself to the boys, including Luke, that saw me through it.

On another evening, Luke came in the classroom looking very upset. I said nothing to him and continued helping the boys with their projects. Luke came up to where I was sitting and stood behind me, breathing down my neck. I just kept helping Leslie with his clay. After a moment or two, I turned around to face him. He looked so angry and yet so wanting. I calmly said, "Come on, Luke. Here's a ball of clay. Come over here and make something out of it."

He followed me to a place at a table all by himself. Trying not to be too obvious, I glanced over to where he was sitting and staring at the five-inch clay ball, pounding on it lightly with his fist. As I approached him, he gave me one of his fiery looks. I leaned close to his shoulder and whispered, "Luke, I think that ball of clay you have is really you." He quickly covered the clay with his hands so I couldn't see it. "You can make something really good out of that clay. I know you can."

"Clay is dumb. It's for sissies," he fired back.

"Well then, Luke, prove yourself. Make something really good out of it, MAN!" I made him angry. He spent the next hour working away with his hands while trying to keep me from seeing what he was making. After the rest of the boys had left, he was still working on his clay. I went about as usual cleaning up the sink and tools. Luke called to me. "Come over here.... There!" he said, expecting to shock me. I looked down at his work and saw that he had made an eight-inch man figure lying flat on the table, dead, with a carving tool stuck in his back.

"That's good Luke. It's a start," was all I said. That wasn't what he expected me to say. Rather than seeing something wrong, I saw promise and let him know it. I wanted him to know that

I understood where he was coming from. Eventually he showed real talent and was an inspiration to the rest of the class.

When I was finally making headway with him, one of the boys told me that Luke and Father Ed had a fight. Father didn't say a thing to us staff about it, but Luke was whisked away the next morning, never to be seen again at the ranch. After Luke was gone, the boys looked up to him and referred to him as Big Luke, as if he was a hero for something he did.

Occasionally Father would get frustrated with a boy who didn't respond well to his brand of counseling, *Whatever that was.* He would turn the boy over to me to work with. After he had told them over and over, "I am your father," it hurt them to be rejected in this way.

This happened to Jim. He was a boy, a young man, sixteen years of age, from Albuquerque. I was informed that he was diabetic, epileptic and suicidal. He had been told by his mother all his life that he would not live another year. Jim believed it. Now that Father was done trying to work with him, Jim was left to me. It wasn't a chore for me, rather it was a gift. Jim and I related well with each other. I found him to be intelligent to the point where I could not "pull the wool" over his eyes on anything. I was honest with him, and he was honest with me.

Often, we would go out for a walk down the road to the creek, while imagining animal shapes in the clouds. It was something I encouraged, to get his thoughts away from his troubled mind. He trusted me even when he felt depressed and alone. Jim would share his despair. He told me how he wanted to kill himself, but he was always afraid to die. He had been to the Bernalillo Medical Center in Albuquerque numerous times; however, he never did well there for any length of time. His mother finally gave up on him, so he was at the ranch. All I could do was encourage him, love him as my brother, and let him know that I would always be there for him. It was a commitment I vowed to honor and I never forgot it.

Months later, it happened. Father Ed was away on his spring begging trip. Tony was in his apartment and I was sitting in the lobby early before the boys were supposed to be up. Suddenly ten-year-old Michael came crashing through the double doors yelling at me. "Hurry, hurry, Jim fell down, I'm scared!"

I jumped up, slammed back the double doors and ran down the long hall to Jim's room. Mike and two older boys were on the floor holding Jim down, while all the time Jim was trying to kick his legs and thrash about. I remembered how Jim had told me, "If I ever start thrashing my legs, it means it's too late. I'm dying." Soon the hall echoed with Jim's terrifying screams, as the boys tried to hold him to keep him from hurting himself. Tony came running from his apartment into the room, recognizing the seriousness of the situation.

"He needs his insulin. Quick, get the one he uses out of his little refrigerator!" Tony shouted to me. I got up off the floor and hurried to the cooler that Jim was allowed to keep in the room. Upon opening it, I saw on the wire shelf two vials of insulin staring me in the face. One vial was cloudy looking, the other one clear.

"Which one, Tony? Tell me which one to pick!" I felt totally helpless. Tony didn't know, Jim was getting worse and I had no one to ask. No one except God. All my life I had prayed respectfully asking for things from God. Now I was on my knees in front of a little refrigerator, not in a church in front of an altar. I had no time for fancy prayers or pleas. With my weakness as my only defense, I didn't ask; I simply said, "It's up to you God. YOU put the right vial in my hand. You have to do it for me."

To this day, I can't recall which vial I took to Tony to give to Jim. Tony administered the injection, and within minutes Jim's body went limp. Together, we carefully moved him onto his bed where he lay motionless on his back without any further sound. Tony returned to his apartment while the boys left to go about their morning chores. Not wanting Jim to wake up alone, I carefully scooted my body up alongside of him on the bed so he would know I was with him should he wake up confused.

I must have lay there motionless for at least two hours. Jim was resting, and I thanked God, as well as apologized for having been so demanding of him. It was about eleven o'clock in the morning when Jim calmly woke up. He simply turned his head to the left, coming within inches of my face. Without any emotion, he looked coldly into my eyes and in a low voice asked, "How did you know?"

The stark question took me back for a moment. I quickly realized what he was referring to. "Jim, I didn't. I told God he had to pick which one, and He did."

Jim held his stare at me for several long moments as if to be checking the truth in my eyes. "The other one would have killed me." With that, he turned his head, closed his eyes, and fell asleep. This incident was never brought up again, but Jim knew then, that two of us would always be there for him.

CHANGING TIMES 4

The boys' ranch motto was, "Fear Checks, Love Corrects." But it seemed that Father Ed's approach to dealing with the boys was limited to using fear to keep the boys in check without showing any love — a twist to the meaning of the motto.

It was even becoming obvious at staff meetings that he didn't care for suggestions from the staff; he only wanted to direct and to control every aspect of how we worked for him. Staff meetings were tense as he used intimidation to squelch any constructive criticism that didn't fit his thinking. Sister Sarah kept her silence, while Sister Mary Carmel, on the other hand, would try to push her points, usually getting nowhere. I used to argue, too, but I turned to typing out long letters to Father, trying to get him to understand that his behavior with everyone was detrimental to the success of the ranch. All the meetings and all the comments about the meetings were carefully noted in my growing collection of note books and journals. Still Father Ed remained stubborn.

No idea I had was ever right. One time he had the boys spreading coal furnace cinders around the trees. Father Ed said it was good for them. I patiently tried to show him that coal cinders were not a form of fertilizer; the acidic cinders would kill the elm trees. Only when Tony talked to him with the same message did he concede and had all the cinders removed. Removing cinders and replacing them with dirt fell into his cynical way of punishing the boys. Besides denying them privileges, or putting everyone on dry cereal for supper, or on some other food restriction, he had boys hauling wheelbarrows full of dirt, sometimes even at night. For example: Get caught with cigarettes from town — six loads of dirt. If you call someone a name — two loads of dirt. Your dorm room is left dirty — everyone hauls dirt.

The older a boy was, the more the loads he had to push. Worse than that, Father would threaten to use his belt, saying, "If a boy causes trouble with any of the women in the kitchen or classrooms, he will get twelve to twenty-four swats with my belt." I never heard of his doing that, but I wasn't around all the time either.

To complain too much about what Father Ed was doing could mean being told to leave the ranch immediately. Father would say to the staff, "You are not their Father, I am. You staff members, do what you are supposed to do — or leave." With that as a constant threat, we all tried hard to put in our one hundred percent for the boys without upsetting Father. If we were to leave, who would be left to help the boys? It was a dilemma, since each of us staff felt we had to stay for the sake of the boys we had come to love. I became totally focused on my work, trusting that God was directing my life, and all would be OK.

During my first few years as a volunteer, I lived on the ranch property in one of the small staff apartments that the Knights of Columbus had built. It was a pleasant apartment. However, as Father Ed was always on the edge of threatening staff with expulsion from the ranch, I decided to look for a place of my own nearby. After months of searching for someone who would sell a Farley town lot to me, I was able to buy a piece of abandoned property directly across the road from the Hacienda fence. The property had a small adobe house, with plenty of space next to it for a mobile home. Mr. Macaroon in Springer, who had helped get used trailers for the ranch to accommodate the Sisters and the cook, now helped me get a used trailer for my property. Having my own place allowed me to be a little more independent of the boys' ranch even while I was still a volunteer there. This arrangement seemed acceptable to Father Ed. In fact, he seemed glad I was away from the ranch property when I was on my own time.

As one year lead into another, I became increasingly frustrated when I would have to change class schedules because Father Ed changed the orders, holding back certain boys from classes: boys who had to report to his room in the evening for counseling, instead of coming to their evening class with me. Other staff were upset as well and felt that their attention to the boys was causing Father to be jealous. He would take his jealousy out on the boys. I could understand why they would try to run away. No doubt they felt picked on and were homesick. All I could do was concentrate on my work, my mission, even if it was under the heavy controlling hand of Father Ed.

But it didn't work out. Eventually, by 1975, Father Ed and I locked horns. I had to finally stand up against his sternness and irregular behavior with the boys. Too many boys were trying to run away. I wrote several more letters to Father Ed, addressing my concerns about him and the ranch, but he resented my comments. He made it impossible for me to have any time with the boys. Without his support, and with too many humiliations from him in front of everyone, I decided that it was time for me to leave the ranch. Father Ed simply announced at the next morning meeting that "Pierre will be leaving the ranch today." That was it. Fortunately, I had my trailer to live in and there I could plan what I would do next. I liked living in New Mexico; I didn't want to go back East, and I still wanted to be close to the ranch. *Maybe Father Ed will soften. Maybe a new director will take over the boys' ranch, then I could return.*

After I left the ranch, I lived a very sparse life across the road from my shattered dreams of helping the boys. The boys weren't happy about my leaving. They were told not to speak a word to me. Nevertheless, we exchanged friendly waves from time to time. I felt like a failure. I had let my principles lead me away from my mission. No longer a volunteer, I was looked down on by others, as if I had done something wrong. I was no longer a part of the ranch and was shunned locally because I had left. With no money or direction in life, I waited and prayed for guidance. *Why, God, has it all come to this? What do you want me to do? Why am I here? Are you even listening?*

I had some good but lonely days. I was in survival mode. I had my little mobile home and life was simple. I felt a certain pride in being able to manage my basic needs. I raised chickens and foraged along the roadside, cutting clover to feed my rabbits. Yes, I missed being with the boys at the ranch. Occasionally, I had the chance to find out something of what was going on over there. New staff would start out, only to leave soon after, like my friend David must have done even before I arrived at the ranch in 1969. It was the same with new boys. It wasn't long before each newly-arrived boy would try to run away. Most of them got caught and brought back to the ranch by the State Highway Patrol. Several managed to never come back. That was the case with Jim. He left one night headed for Albuquerque and went back to living with his mother.

It was a Tuesday morning, January 27, 1976. Father Ed and some of the boys were away on a begging trip, leaving Tony in charge of the ranch. From my house, I noticed something unusual was going on across the road. A State Patrol officer from Springer pulled up in front of the ranch building. After quickly going in and out of the building, the officer left immediately, followed by Tony in the ranch van. Something serious had happened. That afternoon, Peggy Fry, herself an ex-staffer living a block away, came hurrying down the dirt road with her coat carelessly thrown over her shoulders. She came shivering, out of breath, banging on my trailer door.

"Oh Pierre! Two boys took off last night in the cold and ran away. Phillip is in the hospital, but poor Alan is over there at the ranch. He didn't go with them. What will he do when he is told that his little brother, Vaughn, froze to death!"

A freight train was speeding down the rails toward me. I barely saw its hellish light before it hit me in the chest. My heart burst as my mind screamed, hearing those horrible words. "What happened?" I yelled angrily at her, hoping to hear it differently. Again, she choked out the words, that Phillip had survived the cold, but Vaughn, the smaller of the two, had frozen to death overnight somewhere out in the prairie along interstate I-25. *Oh, dear God! What is going on?*

Father Ed returned from his begging trip that night. No

doubt he conferred with Tony on how to do damage control. Peggy Fry caught a hint of an incident that occurred that morning when Tony went in to town with the officer. According to Mrs. Fry who always seemed to have ears and eyes aimed at the ranch across from her window, when Tony first saw Phillip in Springer, just before he was taken to the hospital, he confiscated a small note book in which Phillip had been writing about their whole experience, including why they were running away. The notebook was never given to the authorities. If this was true, it was a cover-up.

The next morning the front gate to the boys' ranch was closed. None of the boys were allowed out of the building for days. All we could find out for sure was that a private funeral for Vaughn would be held at the ranch chapel. Burial would be up north of Farley in the country cemetery of Our Lady of Mount Carmel. Apparently, a plot for Vaughn was granted by the "good Catholic" land owners. Because Vaughn was not a Catholic, they insisted that he would have to be buried outside the fence. What a shameful sight for Vaughn's family to see!

Two days later I happened to meet Tony as he was taking some of the older boys up to the cemetery to dig the grave for Vaughn. Tony and I had been friends over the years. I still considered him a friend even after I left the ranch. Four years earlier, in 1971, I had the honor of being godfather for his newborn daughter, Cecilia Marie, an honor I was never given even by my own married siblings. I took being *"el padrino"* seriously and saw a future with Cecilia, helping to guide her through life. Looking at her smiling face was like looking at an angel. My little baby godchild was the subject of this song I wrote and sang to her at her baptism, and again, one year later.

"Cecilia Marie, close your sleepy eyes. Put your head
  on my shoulder,
I'll hold you close to me. Cecilia Marie, before time
  flies.
Cecilia Marie, see the sky is blue. The swallow sings
  her happy song
And stirs the gentle breeze, Cecilia Marie, just for you.

Cecilia Marie, the sandman's coming soon. Close
  your sleepy eyes,
If you do not cry, I will sing a song to you.
Cecilia Marie, can you hear the things I say, can you
  see me smile
As I think of you in this very special way.

I love you, yes I do, Cecilia Marie.
Promise that when we meet again
That you'll remember me."

One year later, in 1972, after succumbing to complications of Downs Syndrome, our little angel, who had come into this world and won a place in our hearts, was taken back. There was a peace at her funeral; we knew she was back in the arms of pure love. The boys from the ranch had dug her oversized grave. It was a perfectly cut shape in the dry ground. When it came time to lower her little coffin into that huge grave, the men fumbled nervously over how to lower the little treasure box with their ropes. Seeing the awkwardness of the situation, Tony looked over at me as if to alert me to the problem. Without any hesitation and with gasps from a few attendees, I jumped down into the deep grave. The warmth of the sun beaming straight down filled the grave with bright light as if to convey that all was right. Tony knelt at the edge of the opening to carefully lower the beautiful little velvet coffin into my hands. With love from Tony, his wife, their four other children and myself, I kissed the coffin one last time, laid it softly in the wooden crate in which it had come from the mortuary. With a painful look in his eyes, Tony handed down the wooden top of that box, along with a hammer and some nails. My last duty as godfather was to nail shut the wooden lid on the box. That was the hardest thing to do. The sound of it seemed to signal the end of a dream. Cecilia Marie was gone.

Now, as I saw Tony and the boys again heading to that cemetery, was the beginning of another heartbreak, another hole to be dug little more than five feet from my Cecilia Marie. After Tony drove off to get the grave dug for Vaughn, I couldn't help feeling angry with myself. I was supposed to be there across the road still with the ranch, still involved with helping Father Ed. I believed in him. The rumors couldn't be true. I should have been next to Father to help sort it all out. If there was something bad going on, I mean really bad that Father was doing, surely the caseworker from Raton would have heard of it from the boys she interviewed over the years. My head was spinning with conflict. I couldn't think it all out. Father was a priest. He wouldn't do anything wrong with the boys. I always trusted him.

The day of Vaughn's funeral came all too soon. There was a private ceremony held at the ranch chapel that cold January morning. Meantime, I drove up to the cemetery by myself and waited as inconspicuously as I could while people began to arrive. Some local ranchers came, but only a few people from town. I doubted that Father Ed gave any public notice of what had happened.

Soon the Garcia family along with Father Ed and some of the boys, arrived. No one talked at all or asked any questions. It was obvious Father Ed was nervous as he fussed uncomfortably with the Roman collar around his neck. I remember it well, as I too stood silently waiting for the hearse to arrive. Finally, the shiny black limousine came down the dirt road and crossed through the opened barbed wire gate. It looked out of place, swaying heavily side to side, trying to cross with dignity to the cemetery through the rutted prairie grass. The vehicle stopped in front of the little white Our Lady of Mount Carmel Church. Minutes later Vaughn's family got out. Assisted by the funeral director, they made their way into the cemetery. Passing around the big wooden cross, they slowly walked through the patchwork of tombstones and took their places before Vaughn's grave. I noticed their worn clothing. No doubt it was the best they had for this sad occasion. Alan, Vaughn's brother, stood motionless to the right of his mother. His two little sisters cuddled near "Mamma" at her left, as she held them tightly to her side.

Father Ed was nervous as he proceeded with his official priestly duties. No song was sung, no lengthy eulogy, only silence. It was so unlike last year when over there in the nearby junipers we were sharing fun and laughter with the boys at our Easter egg hunt. All the while, I looked at Vaughn's mother. Her eyes told a story of sadness, as if all her trust in the ranch and all her hopes for Vaughn were lost.

Procession time came; feet dragged heavily through the dusty dirt in a line towards the silvery casket deep in the grave. Each mourner did the ritual. Like robots on a conveyer belt, each dropped his handful of soil on the coffin. The dirt landed in a splash of gravel and a thud that seemed disrespectful. No doubt the crumbly clay fell each time accompanied by a prayer for Vaughn.

I could feel only sadness. I thought of this young boy and my own journey to meet him, to help him. I wrestled fearfully with my thoughts. *Was I part of what failed Vaughn? What happened to cause this thirteen-year-old boy to lose his life?* Reluctantly, I held the clump of clay in my shaking hand. My thoughts were broken by Mrs. Fernandez, nudging me along, whispering to me in her gentle voice, "Go ahead now, just let go. Just let go." My hand opened and my bomb of dirt fell on target. With it went a solemn promise. *To you Vaughn, I swear I will find out why you had to run away. Why you had to die.*

THE START 5

efore I moved to New Mexico, I knew very little about the state. Growing up in Chicago and the suburbs gave me a rather myopic awareness of places outside of my local life. Now I was here by myself, in the prairie lands of northeast New Mexico, living off the money I made from selling my belongings back in Ohio. I had come to enjoy the outdoors: hunting, trail biking and exploring. I even enjoyed the challenges of the winter blizzards that would roll across the open plains with little warning. But now, even as things settled down after Vaughn's funeral, I couldn't seem to enjoy anything.

I wrestled every night over the situation across the road at the Hacienda de los Muchachos Boys Ranch. I knew I had to do something; I had made a graveside promise. Sometimes I wanted to forget about it all, yet I couldn't let it go without some resolution. But what could I do? Where could I start to search for the answers to why Phillip and Vaughn ran away? I certainly wasn't going to confront Father Ed. I suspected he would have a lot of questions to answer from the state agencies and other authorities. I couldn't dare give him cause to suspect that I too might be questioning him. No, if I was going to do any inquiring, it would have to be on my own. Still, I could not rest at night. I struggled with the confusion over what had just happened. I knew I could not wait any longer worrying about the "what ifs." I had to start searching for answers on my own.

Occasionally I would have the chance to chat with Tony, Father Ed's assistant at the ranch across the road. We maintained a friendship even after I left the ranch. It was little over a month after Vaughn's funeral when I was talking with him that he mentioned how the boys really missed those trips I use to take them on to Ute Creek. Robert in particular always seemed to talk about it. Suddenly, like the proverbial switch of a light bulb, an idea flashed in my head.

"If it would be OK with you, Tony," I asked, "I'd like to take Robert down to the creek as a treat."

"Well, I guess that would be OK. Father Ed is away on a begging trip, so go ahead."

"We'll only be gone a short while, and I know Robert will have a really good time. I'll pick him up right after today's siesta." My heart began pounding like a drum as I sensed the opportunity I would have to talk to Robert. He was fifteen years old. His younger brother was there at the ranch also. Neither of them were run-a-ways; they had been at the ranch for several years. Robert, as much as any other boy, would probably know what might be going on behind Father Ed's blue door.

As soon as I got back in the house, I started to type out questions and made a list of things I hoped Robert would talk about. I felt confident that he would share the truth without my asking prying questions. It would be a delicate conversation. I wanted to show support for him while not saying anything bad about Father Ed. He did not need to know what I was really up to.

Three o'clock came and there was Robert out on the road in

front of the ranch building. His big cheesy smile made me feel relaxed and happy to see him again. He hopped into my old jeep, and away we went down the dirt road to Ute Creek. We had our special spots the boys liked, such as the ice jumping place, and the one near the rock ledge where we always looked for arrowheads.

"Where do you want to stop?" I called out to Robert, as we drove down the road along the creek.

"Keep going!" he yelled back, laughing and having a great time. Further up, where the old Santa Fe trail crossed the creek, was a good place to stop, and so we did.

"First one to the creek wins," I called out. After hunting arrowheads and throwing rocks in the water, we settled down on the sandy side of the creek bed to enjoy some cookies I'd brought along.

"Robert, may I ask you some things about what it is like for you with Father and the ranch?"

With his big grin pushed close to my face, he tilted his head comically to the side and replied, "That would be OK. I don't mind."

I thought it significant that he seemed to want to say something to me. At first, we talked about past fun times and recalled events that he should remember well, such as the time we were down at the Gonzalez's ranch, hiking around Miera Butte and found that cool coyote skull. Each thing I brought up, Robert remembered all the details right away.

With that check of his memory, I opened my folder and began with the easiest questions. Every answer that Robert gave, I recorded exactly as he gave it to me. We talked about the differences between right and wrong, and also about what responsibility meant. Then came the details of what had been done to him and other boys behind the Blue Door in Father Ed's private bedroom. Had I not been so focused on getting his words written down, I think the full meaning of what he was saying would have made it impossible for me to go on maintaining calm. Robert was very graphic in his descriptions of the sexual abuse he and the other boys had to endure.

"It wasn't wrong," Robert said, "because he is our Father. Father told us that. We had to call him Father every time or else we would be punished. He called us his sons all the time. When he had us in his room he said, 'Now I'm going to show you how much I love you,' then he would do it."

"Do what. Robert?" I asked. Robert began to describe how Father Ed would have boys into his room where he would use them with his hands and his mouth. Robert's descriptions were horrifyingly graphic. "He would force his finger inside of me at the same time and it hurt."

"Did everyone have to do it with him or was it only his 'Special Pets'?"

"He has special boys he favors. If one didn't do it, he'd put him on restrictions or take his food away."

"That's not a very nice way to show love, is it, Robert?"

"No," Robert said. "I keep telling my little brother not to go into Father's room at night, but he does. He is scared that Father will hurt him, so he will do anything. My poor brother."

"Are you scared of Father Ed?" I asked.

"Yes! He could take his belt off and hit you on the head with the buckle where it wouldn't show, if you didn't do something for him. Then say it was an accident."

"This is very, very serious talk you know, Robert. God is very unhappy with wrong and evil. We cannot make things up or tell lies about this. Do you understand?"

"Yes, because God is listening. I know and I pray at night for God to help Vaughn 'cause maybe He'll say, "That's all right, Vaughn. You can come to heaven, I forgive you. Someone prayed for you.""

My heart broke from sadness as I heard Robert, a boy who himself had been so abused, showing such compassion for his lost friend, Vaughn.

"Did Father Ed do those things with every boy?" I asked.

"No, not everyone. Mostly only with us older boys," Robert said, "but not so much with the younger boys. Father didn't like them because, how do you say it, they weren't developed. They didn't have hair yet."

I asked, "Did Father ever give alcohol, money, or favors if a boy did everything he asked of him?"

"Yes," was always the answer.

"I heard that after I left the ranch, Father Ed changed his back room in his private quarters into what he called his "Skin Room."

Robert was quick to say, "Oh, that's where, if you've been good, you can get to go in there at night and watch TV."

"But why," I continued, "was it called the skin room?"

With a bit of excitement in his voice, Robert said, "He has these neat furs all over the floor, and we all lie on them to watch TV."

"Do you mean the boys on the furs? Where did Father Ed watch TV?"

"Oh, he was on the floor too," Robert said.

"When your name was on the afternoon list, telling who was going to get to watch TV, how did you dress to go in his room come evening?"

"Father said we had to wear only our underwear, that's all."

"How is he dressed when you or another boy is in his room? Does he have clothes on all the time, or never, or what?" I asked.

"Oh, Father doesn't have any clothes on either."

"Was Father and the things he did to boys, the reason the boys wanted to run away?"

"Always," Robert said.

After a long pause, I asked him the critical questions that had been eating away at me night and day.

"Some of these things you say Father did? Was that why Phillip and Vaughn ran away?"

"Yes," Robert said "They didn't want to do it with him. Are you going to do something about this, Pierre? I wish I could talk. I wish I could do something to help."

"You cannot Robert, because you are not of age." I replied.

"Boy, wait until I'm old enough! Boy, I'll tell everything I know just like I told you."

All I could offer Robert at the moment was, "Let's hope for your brother's sake and others too, that it won't go on much longer."

Robert's honesty made my hand shake as I wrote down all the terrible things he continued to tell me. When I heard these things and all the awful details, I felt myself falling head first into Dante's Hell; my heart sank in the fire of my anger. *How to quench the pain? When comes the Phoenix?* With all said, we agreed not to tell anyone about our talk. I wanted to give Robert a reassuring hug, but after hearing how he had been manipulated and violated, I couldn't do it. I felt cheated by what Father Ed had done, even to me. With that, it was over.

"Let's go throw some more stones," I said.

"Watch me!" Robert shouted, as he skipped a pebble across the creek.

"Rocks always make cool ripples, don't they Pierre." I couldn't help thinking about my pebbles in life, skipping dangerously across the waters. "How many times do you think this stone will skip before it reaches the other side?" Robert called again.

"You never know until you try," I replied, repeating it over again in my mind several times. We spent the last of our time at the creek searching for interesting rocks, arrowheads, and sharing the last of our cookies. Robert was ready for the jeep ride back to the ranch. I drove slowly so as to make the last minutes of the ride last longer for Robert's enjoyment.

When we arrived, he was beaming with pride in front of the other boys for the special outing he had just been on. "That was so much fun," he said and gave me his last big goofy smile. I had a hard time holding back my emotions. I couldn't help feeling that I was releasing him into the mouth of a shark, back into a horrible situation with which he had to cope to survive. Anger fueled my Dantesque fire with a vengeance. *How could someone do such terrible things to children?*

Another sleepless night. I poured over the notes I'd taken, carefully typing them out as a record of everything both of us had said. I felt so drained, so weak as I looked forward to where this was leading me. Because of a promise to Vaughn this started, but now it was becoming much more. *Oh God, give me the strength to know the way.*

The next day the sun was out bright and warm. I felt energized. I was going to see my dear friend Mary to break the story to her. I knew she would be a help. Mary and Francis Hefner were my best ranch friends. Over the years, I felt almost as if we were family — genuine, loving friends they were to me. They were Catholic and had raised children themselves, so I felt confident they would understand what I was doing. The closer I got to their place near Gladstone, the worse I felt. My emotions were building up uncontrollably. I didn't want to look distraught. *Get it together,* I said to myself.

When I walked into the front room where Mary was sitting and watching her afternoon TV program, she turned her swivel chair around to greet me. Seeing my jaw quivering with emotion, she blurted out, "Oh, Pierre, did your father die?"

"No, Mary, it's not that." I laughingly replied back, as if

that wouldn't have qualified. "It's something else even worse." She got up, gave me a much-needed hug, and motioned for me to sit down. Surrendering willingly, I poured myself into the warm afghan-covered recliner, as she turned off the TV to give me her full attention.

"Mary, there is something I have to talk to you about. I can't carry it alone. Please help me." Francis came in the room from the barn and quickly found a place to sit down, having gotten a nod and the "do it now" look from Mary.

"Tell me, Pierre, what is it?" she said with the softness only a mother knows how to give.

With a deep breath and a bit of consternation, I proceeded to spill my story out to them. As I talked, I could see Mary's face changing from her usual plump smile to a drawn, almost sickly look. Once she began to read the interview I did with Robert, she couldn't keep from covering her mouth with her hand, as if to hold back words of anger over what it all meant. Francis looked over the material while Mary sat silently, rocking in her chair. Both Mary and Francis had known Father Ed for years and were dumbfounded by what they were now learning about him. As I had hoped, they completely believed Robert's answers. Mary looked over to Francis for his reaction. He wasted no time saying, "It's terrible. How can we help, Pierre?" That was the beginning of many hours and many dollars they gave to help me along the way.

That night, Mary wouldn't let me go home without having supper. It was the first decent meal I'd had in a long time. Francis and Mary were simple farm folks and I loved every little quirk I saw in them. They were the only friends I had. Francis was farm-raised as a child; Mary was a town girl from Clayton. They shared their life stories with me many times. As a child, Francis had seen his mother die in the cold of winter. He said that Vaughn's death reminded him of that time long ago when influenza was taking so many lives. "The snow was so deep at the farm," Francis said, "and the weather was so cold, all my father could do was wrap up Mother in a blanket and lay her outside on the cold north side of the house in the snow. Once the weather let up, he took her into town." Francis too had pain to share. I felt privileged to be there to console him in return.

The next days at home were a reprieve. I drove to Ute creek to walk along the grassy edge. I wanted things to still be good and simple the way I once thought they were, but never really were. I had to face that reality. It was a different Ute Creek now. It was a different everything now. I thought about Robert skipping stones. It was my turn. Reaching down I found my stone. I was ready.

NO STOPPING NOW 6

Although I certainly believed what Robert told me, I knew I would need more evidence of sexual abuse by Father Ed. I needed another interview with a boy who had been at the ranch. An older boy who was with Tony the day they went to dig Vaughan's grave had said something about a buddy who had run away from the ranch two years earlier. He told Tony that his friend was now living in Las Vegas, New Mexico, and working as a laborer doing roofing. Tony had mentioned this to me so I knew to whom he was referring. I decided to see if I could find him. I drove down to Las Vegas and checked the phone book for a roofing company. I waited near that business to see when the workers would be returning from their job.

About 5:30 P.M., two trucks pulled into the company lot. Four guys climbed out of their vehicles with their coats and coolers. I immediately recognized the boy whom I wanted to see. He looked tired — a man now, with the look of premature aging often found in the less fortunate who struggle through life. When he first saw me, he looked scared, as if to say, *"Leave me alone."* When I extended my hand to greet him, he put his work-dirty hand in mine. I could feel no strength in his grasp, as if it all had been used up. His eyes gave way to an expression of deep wanting, almost as if he'd been waiting for me. It gave me a strange feeling that my Jesus had been there earlier, helping to bring us together again.

I didn't know him well when he was at the ranch, however

I remembered that he fell from grace with Father over something and ran away the next day. It was going to be a difficult visit trying to convince him that I, we, needed to do something to stop Father Ed. He motioned for me to follow him to the far side of the truck where no one could see us. I told him about Vaughn, about Robert, and about how I needed his help to confirm what Robert had said. It made him feel very nervous. He looked down, shaking his head slowly, indicating to me that he was recalling some of his own painful past. He insisted, "Before I tell you anything, I want you to promise me that you will never use my name. I would rather die than tell this to anyone else." I promised to honor his request; I have never used his name.

I took him out for dinner at a local restaurant where we could sit and talk. After we had eaten, I tried to bring up some of the fun things we did at the ranch, but he didn't seem to want to talk about that. When I took out my prepared folder of questions, he sat up straight in the booth, indicating to me that he was ready for the serious part of our meeting. Everything he said about how he was abused, mentally and physically, deepened the seriousness of the situation at the boys' ranch. He told me, "Everyone was scared of being beaten with Father's belt when no staff were around. We were afraid to sleep at night for fear of his coming and taking us in the dark to his room. We had no choice. Sometimes he would give us alcohol to get us drunk so he could have his way hurting us, while saying how special we were to him."

"What kind of alcohol was he giving to you?" I asked.

"Sometimes it was only altar wine that he gave me. Other times, depending on how Father liked you, it would be the hard liquor that he kept in his bedroom. Don was his most trusted boy. He got to serve us the drinks. Father gave Don money all the time."

"How do you suppose Father Ed got the liquor to give to you?"

The young man lowered his head again, as if reflecting on the answer he was about to give. He said, "I liked Mr. Garcia. He wasn't mean to me like Father Ed was. Sometimes Mr. Garcia, or Tony as we sometimes called him when Father wasn't around, would let us older boys have a beer from his apartment. One time when I was in Father's room, Tony delivered some bottles of liquor to Father. I guess that's how Father got his stuff to give to us. We had to do what Father said. If we fought back, he wouldn't let us go to school in Springer, and he would make things worse for us around the ranch. The only one who ever fought back was Luke. They got in a real fight. I remember it," he continued. "Father Ed said something to Luke; Luke hauled off and punched Father Ed in the face, knocking him down butt naked to the floor."

"Was that why they called him Big Luke?" I asked.

"Yeah, but we all paid the price, as Father Ed showed us who was boss. He took it out on us. We had no one we could talk to — too scared. He could kill anyone of us. Anyhow that's the way we all felt."

That this young man had been able to survive the physical and mental abuse was a credit to his perseverance. I could tell it left him feeling alone in life. He had no family that wanted him. He was a man all by himself. All I could do was help him realize that if he told me the full truth he could help stop the abuse that was still going on at the ranch. His descriptions and personal experiences made Robert's account sound like a walk in the park. Father Ed's deceptiveness and the control he had over the boys was so powerful that, as this young man said, it was life threatening. This was the final straw. I had enough documentation now.

A week later, when I was peeking through the corner of my window toward the ranch building, I realized I was becoming paranoid. Every time I heard a truck or I saw someone different at the ranch, I thought someone was going to find out about me and get me! *Calm down*, I had to say to myself. *No one knows what I've been doing. Or do they?*

My concern elevated when late one night, I looked out my trailer window and noticed vehicle lights at my driveway gate. I heard a door open, then someone got out. After a few seconds, the person got back in the vehicle and drove away in a hurry. This was very unusual as no one ever drove around Farley at night; or would be stopping at my house. After a few quiet moments of standing in the dark, I walked down to the gate to see if anything was different. There, on the post under a rock, was a folded piece of paper. Once back in the house I was alarmed to read, "You might need some protection," written on it; nothing else. I momentarily dismissed it thinking, *Oh, no. I'm fine.* Then putting lie to my thoughts, I went right away and wedged the chair against the handle on the front door, turned out the lights and went to bed. Yes, it scared me as I thought, *what if someone is going to hurt me? Am I in danger?* That night I couldn't sleep. Every creak of the trailer roof startled me. Every brush of the tree or wind against the window kept me awake with concern. *I can't stop now. Jesus protect me.*

Shortly after that, I found out that the State Social Services Agency was finally on Father's back over his defiant statement: "I, Father Ed, will have all the boys I want at the ranch; orphan, troubled, and retarded, you have no say." Of course, this didn't sit well with the agency; they would not allow him to house together boys who were handicapped along with ones who were sent there by the court because of disciplinary problems. The state agency was trying to shut him down by revoking his lease on the old Farley school building. This started an all-out legal battle with Father Ed.

While I was plotting my next clandestine move, Father Ed had as many as four lawyers representing him. He was writing his monthly newsletters to donors, taking in money, and still going on begging trips. All of this was to fire up support for himself and his Hacienda boys' ranch. I was beginning to think that maybe he would win. *That scoundrel!* I had to do more and do it faster.

It wasn't easy for me to be brave. I had never been one to step forward for anything important. As a little kid, I was scared of the chalk board in school. I was afraid to get up in front of everyone and write something wrong, or worse than that, break the new stick of chalk. Here I was, spring of 1976, still scared, confronting another situation. Funny how things keep coming back.

I sensed the need for some spiritual support. I decided to see the new parish priest, Father Jones, at St. Joseph Catholic Church in

Springer. I had met him several times on weekends after I left the boys' ranch. Now I felt confident that he might help. At the very least, I would have shared my worries with a priest. I gathered up all my material, two interviews, and my old journals from the ranch. Those little journals I had written now corroborated my memory of who was allowed to go to the creek and who was to report to Father's room at night. The journals were becoming a backup for some of what the two boys had said.

When I got to the church in Springer, Father Jones invited me into his office where we each told a little about ourselves to "break the ice." At this time, he knew nothing of what I was about to share with him. I reminded him that I had worked with Father Ed not too long ago. Father Jones told me that he himself was now the new chaplain at the New Mexico Boys' School. That was the same facility where Father Ed had been the chaplain before he left to start his own boys' ranch. This revelation made me nervous. I wondered whether I should share this bombshell with him. *What if he sympathized with Father Ed?*

"Father, I need your prayers for the courage and strength to continue with this research I'm doing. I would like you to read it and tell me what you think I should do next with it. I also ask that this meeting and information be covered under the seal of confession."

He agreed, saying, "Yes, of course." With full trust in him, I handed over the thick folder. He began to read. I sat there motionless in my chair trying not to make it squeak. It had to be the longest twenty minutes I'd ever experienced. It was worse than waiting my turn at the dentist when I was a kid. I expected any moment for a burst of emotion from Father. Instead, after long minutes of silence, he slowly closed the folder and set it on the desk. Lowering his head down to where I couldn't see his eyes, he said, "That 'skin room' mentioned here? I remember some of the boys at the State School here in Springer telling me about that, how a few years ago, Father Ed had a 'Blue Room' before he and Mr. Garcia left to start their own facility." I said nothing, waiting for the next words to come from his sad face. Raising his eyes to me he asked, "Would you be afraid to take this to the Archbishop of Santa Fe?"

I panicked, wanting to get up and run away before I was struck by the powerful lightning of the Church. *Me going before an Archbishop? Oh Jesus, this is getting confusing. Which side are you on?* Amazing how much thought can fit in the time frame of a second. Then I surprised myself as I replied to Father, "No, I'm not afraid. Will you go with me, Father Jones?"

"Of course, I have something I need to say also," he replied.

I left the rectory that morning with my material; I was excited. It was a beautiful sunny sky. No lightning yet. I felt good.

It was a long week of waiting before Father Jones could get an appointment with Archbishop Sanchez. During that time, I spent my days typing out for the archbishop a long introductory letter which I would take with me to present to him at his office. Along with that letter was the manila envelope bulging with all my other documentation, including a transcript of Robert's talk with me down at Ute Creek and of the interview I did with the young man in Las Vegas. I closed that introductory letter to the Archbishop with the following words:

My archbishop, to whom I confess in all truthfulness

this material, I beg, for the sake of Father Ed's soul and those dozens of children he may have so wrongly affected, I beg you to act quickly and effectively.

Prayerfully submitted,

Pierre L. Nichols

Finally, the day came for the appointment: February 20th, 1976, thirty-eight days after Vaughn died. I drove to Springer wearing my best jeans and shirt, and brought with me all my material and the introductory letter. Father Jones had a nice car, and it was a pleasant ride south. On the way, down to Albuquerque, we talked lightly about different things. Father told me that his hobby was photography, so I shared how I had been a photographer. I finally had to ask him about how to greet an archbishop. A few years ago, when I first got to the Hacienda boys' ranch, Father Ed took me along on a day trip to Albuquerque so I could meet the then, Archbishop James Davis. I was ready to kiss his ring respectfully upon meeting him, since I'd heard that was what we Catholics should do. But Father Ed and the archbishop simplified it with just a hand shake. Now, I was asking Father Jones about this new, much younger archbishop, Robert Sanchez.

"What should I do?"

Father Jones seemed to chuckle to himself as he answered me, saying, "Archbishop Sanchez doesn't do the ring thing. Just call him Father." *Well that was a relief, but calling an archbishop Father?* Once we got to the archdiocesan offices, I began to feel intimidated by the grandeur of it all. I felt apprehensive sitting in the waiting area. Everything was happening too fast. I began to doubt myself. *Was Father Jones leading me to the slaughter?*

What had I gotten myself into with an archbishop? He wasn't going to be a happy man after he meets me. I could be in real trouble.

Then the devil started messing with my imagination. I could see that big door opening and Archbishop Sanchez in a white robe, levitating through the clouds as angels sang, "Jesus Christ, Super Star." A nudge from Father Jones rescued me from my wandering thoughts just as the mystery door opened. Out came a slight figure of a man dressed in black. No clouds, no angels, only a priest.

"I'm Father Sanchez, pleased to meet you." I was relieved by his warm hand shake; I felt pain over the thought that I was about to dump trouble on him.

After we were all seated in the bishop's office, Father Jones simply said to Archbishop Sanchez, "Pierre has something he wants to share with you."

The ball was in my court. I got up from my seat and tried to force a smile on my face as I handed my introductory letter and the heavy folder to him. I sat back in the plush chair grabbing tight, the arm rests like a kid on a roller coaster, waiting for the first drop to happen. He glanced across his large desk at Father Jones, as if asking, *"what is this?"* With a concerned raise of his hand to his face, he began to read. The longer he read, the worse his face looked. His right hand seemed to move instinctively upward with a finger pointed, like Adam's hand in Michelangelo's fresco, to touch his Creator for some strength.

When he finally closed the folder, he looked as if he had seen a ghost. By this time, anger was building up in my mind as I mulled over what he must be reading. After minutes of total silence, he carefully laid the last of my documentation down on his desk. With a glazed look in his eyes, he said to me, "I'll look into it."

I jumped up from my chair and burst out, "No, Father, you have to do something now! Every day, every night that you don't, Father Ed is there still having boys. It's on your conscience. Do something." I was pointing my finger, staring directly into his eyes as my voice cracked. I saw my hand was shaking, but I didn't care. *Come on, hit me with your lightning.* "I leave it to you, Father Sanchez, Archbishop. Stop Father Ed!"

It took a few minutes of silence for us — especially me — to calm down. Archbishop Sanchez said something to Father Jones, and I guess that meant the meeting was over. Polite handshakes and a blessing, and I was out of his office, folder in hand. Father Jones stayed behind with the Archbishop for his own reasons.

After that, Father Jones and I went out to eat. All I could think of on the way home was that my ordeal and responsibilities were over. I had finished my task by telling the truth to the Archbishop. It was now in his hands, and I felt relieved. Vaughn and the other boys would be vindicated. I couldn't wait to tell Francis and Mary all about it.

FINAL DAYS 7

When you achieve a goal, or feel you can put something behind you — then it often becomes clear that some things don't have an ending. I got back from that trip to Albuquerque feeling relieved, but still I had my worries and concerns for the boys at the ranch. I decided to start writing letters to anyone who could help close the ranch. I got all the local property owners to sign a petition requesting that the ranch be closed because they feared vandalism by runaway boys. I wrote to John Kearney, Director of the State Health Agency and detailed the dilapidated condition of the old school building and gave this as a reason to deny Father Ed a renewal of the lease. In February 1976, I sent a letter to Archbishop Sanchez; in March, a letter to Social Services, Health and Human Services Department of Colfax County; in August, letters to U.S. Senator Pete Domenici, and Governor Jerry Apadaca — all in an effort to focus on closing the ranch for reasons other than the one I had told the archbishop. I was trusting him to take care of Father Ed and to avoid a church scandal. How much coordination went on behind the scenes, I never knew.

By mid-summer, the Hacienda staff was down to only Mr. and Mrs. Garcia. The two Sisters, Sarah and Mary Carmel, had returned to their Mother House in Massachusetts. Mrs. Garcia took over cooking after Irene left. Father Ed found out that the Social Services Agency in Raton was about to come to the ranch and pick up their boys to relocate them, either to other appropriate facilities or back to their parents. As soon as Father Ed was aware of this, he loaded most of the remaining boys in his van and took them to their family homes. In that way, he broke state agency custody. Most of the boys, but not all of them.

Mrs. Fry, who lived across the street from the south wing of the Hacienda, could see the row of dorm windows, including Father Ed's room window, across the road from her house. Though most of the boys were gone, one dorm room light, as well as Father Ed's room light, were still on every night. She said there were at least two boys that he kept back for himself. Day after day, Father Ed or a boy would go out to a burn barrel in front of the building, spending time burning papers from his office. This was a clear sign that things weren't going well for him; he was "cleaning house."

I saw some of this and wondered what the archbishop was doing about the situation. I wrote to him again in June, expressing my concern, repeating what I said to him in person when we had met in Albuquerque in February.

I started the long, five-page letter with *Dear Archbishop Robert Sanchez*. In this letter, I described incidents such as Alan's — Vaughan's brother — choosing not to run away that fateful day and Father Ed's trying to take Alan east on a begging trip to show him off even after his little brother had frozen to death. I wrote to encourage the bishop while reminding him of his responsibilities. Continuing the letter, I wrote;

> My mind turns over dozens of boys' and adults' names who had been treated wrongly by Father Ed. While I will not judge him for his part, still I will fight for a full and permanent solution to the activities that go on at the ranch involving Father

Ed. Archbishop, you are the shepherd of many and yet in your own personal life I'm sure you have many situations where you recognize your effect.... calling, to just one lost sheep at a time. Christ causes this in each of us who listen, I know. I do not have a flock, and my responsibilities are rarely heavy as Christ usually doesn't demand a lot from me, but I have a love for those boys, those souls I keep thinking of. No wolf will feed upon my little brothers again! I guess a new demand has been put upon me this year. One that says, follow through Pierre, turn over the stones, beat the thickets, do what Christ wants done. Help bring about a return to what is right with our brothers. How will you handle it, Father Sanchez? Would you leave the stones unturned or one single soul to perish in the thickets...one small boy in the darkness and fear of a sick Father Ed? No, I know you wouldn't. I know you will act as Christ would. This is why I have faith in your ability to intervene and solve for the sake of the Church and many others, the problems of Father Ed, before legal proceedings begin.

I would like to call your office about June 23-24th, to ask you of your decision and outline for instrumenting it. Perhaps this may be the last letter I'll write to you concerning this matter. I pray earnestly that it will be so.

My archbishop, except my humble prayers and these efforts of help. Christ chose me to carry a part of this task through unqualified as I am, I have tried to do my best. Again, I say, it is in your hands.

Sincerely, Pierre Nichols

(I never received a reply.)

In the meantime, I could see that very little was going on at the ranch. Feeling fairly confident that the archbishop would clean up the situation soon, I worried about Tony. I thought that Tony might be having some concerns about his family and his job at the ranch. Father Ed was under fire, doing what looked like a close out of the Hacienda de los Muchachos Boys Ranch.

One morning, I caught Tony on the road in front of my place as he was driving by. I had to say something to him. I couldn't tell him what I had been up to, but I could warn him to please take care of his family because the boys' ranch was definitely going to close. He looked angrily at me, shouting, "No! The ranch is not going to close. Father will win his case!" I could see anxiety in his eyes, almost a look of fear. I repeated, "Please, Tony, be ready for a move."

"No!" was his answer as he abruptly drove away. I felt bad that I couldn't help him. I could take being rejected by the locals and by the supporters of the boys' ranch — they all thought poorly of me for not supporting Father Ed — but losing Tony's friendship really hurt.

Even though I still had my "Little House on the Prairie," I was beginning to feel a financial squeeze. I had been able to sustain myself over the years by selling off my Ohio belongings —the lake property in Pennsylvania, the sailboat, antiques, etc. I also did some house painting and bucked hay locally to earn some income. When the cash ran out, things got tight. I either had to apply for food stamps or go hungry.

I remember the first time I drove to Raton with my coupon book. I was self-conscious at the supermarket. Like a kid in a candy store, I kept going through the aisles looking at all the extra things that I could now get. I had been living on the barest of essentials. Now I could have real food! When my carefully chosen items were bagged at the checkout, I raised my eyes to the cashier and embarrassed myself completely by saying, "Thank you so much for this." It was a humbling experience.

It was strange for me to think that this was where I was in life. I wasn't complaining; it was the strangeness of it all. I was nowhere at this point. *Should I stay for the final dying days of the boys' ranch, or sell out quickly and get the heck out of Dodge?* I wanted a change. I needed a change. Yet the change I most needed to see was the end of the boys' ranch, including the end of Father Ed. I never damned the man. Oh, for sure I despised him and worked to bring him down, but, thankfully, even to this day, never have I wished to judge him as only God can do. God will gaze, come Judgment Day, at what Father Ed did to "the least of my little ones," and that judgment will be Father Ed's fate. I have no need or desire to add anything to it.

Discernment takes time. I didn't see Tony much, only occasionally when he would drive by with his family in his station wagon. Word in the area was that the last of Father Ed's lawyers had withdrawn from his case. I even saw Archbishop Sanchez at the ranch one day. I was in front of my trailer and noticed a shiny car pulling up to the front of the Hacienda. When he waved to me, I recognized the archbishop. I thought for certain that he was there to tell Father to vacate. But I neither saw nor heard of any change. *How long can this go on?*

It was now August, three months since my last letter to

Archbishop Sanchez and six months since I showed him the evidence at his office. I wrote Archbishop Sanchez again, asking him to stop Father Ed from having even one boy with him. Whether it was because of him or the state or something else, word finally came in 1977 that the ranch was going to close. There was to be a huge auction in several weeks of all the contents of the building. After that, the Hacienda de los Muchachos would no longer exist.

Meanwhile, Father Ed was moving stuff into a small house in town and passing out things to favored ranchers who had supported him over the years. Tony was also moving his family's belongings from the ranch building. In three days, he and his family were gone. He never stopped to say goodbye to me. He seemed to be in a hurry to get away, possibly out of New Mexico.

With an auction at the ranch coming soon, I decided I didn't want to stay around to watch people divide up the remnants of the ranch. What would become of all the ceramics the boys had made, of all the arrowheads that Father had taken from them, of all the objects that had meaning for me? *Let them have it, I don't care.* I decided the best thing for me was to get away from it all. Time to try something different.

WHICH ROAD? 8

I heard about a facility near Pecos, New Mexico, where they worked with special needs adults. *Perhaps I could be a volunteer there?* When I checked into it, I found out that this facility was also being investigated for alleged physical abuse. I began to realize that putting down the Hacienda de los Muchachos Boys Ranch as my work experience wasn't going to look good on any application in New Mexico.

My next thoughts turned to manual labor, somewhere far away from all I had seen and heard. I found that laborers were needed in the Colorado cantaloupe fields, so I decided to try that. At least it would be a simple job. *Who knows, maybe even a calling in a new direction?* I packed my jeep, locked up the trailer for the summer, and headed to Rocky Ford, Colorado, and a new way of life. It felt good to be away from New Mexico, even if my new work home was a dingy little motel room I rented for the summer. The next morning, I drove over to a "Laborers Wanted" sign near a field just out of town. A big weathered-looking man with a straw hat came hurrying toward me and asked, "*Hablas Español?*"

"No."

"Then you go now with them others over there," he said with a look of disgust. I walked over to where other workers were waiting next to a flatbed truck. Immediately I felt self-conscious, dressed in new jeans and a short-sleeved shirt. Everyone else was clothed in weather-faded long-sleeved shirts and straw hats. I had a lot to learn about surviving in the fields. After years of working with disadvantaged children I was now working with disadvantaged adults. *Could this be my new calling?* I wasn't going to drive a truck or be in charge of anything, as I had thought I might. Instead, I was going to be picking melons, like the other men and women who quietly accepted their fate in life.

That afternoon, the sun felt hot and heavy as molten lead on the back of my neck. Face down, stooped over in the rows picking the vines, was not what I expected. But fate, like that burning sun, sometimes bears down and weathers dreams and bends the backs of better men than I. Cheap machinery was what we had been reduced to in that field — Mexican families and transient workers all mixed together for survival. I was one of them, with sore back and sore hands from loading melons. Next to me was a dark-skinned woman who couldn't speak English and who rarely looked over to me, other than to cut me to the quick with her sharp eyes. I decided right then, that she was one of those foreigners whom I wasn't going to like; after all, I wasn't the alien — or was I? She always seemed irritated with me, as if I weren't doing my job fast enough. When she could see me struggling with the melons, she would try to hide her smile.

"Gringo, el no sabe nada!" I heard someone say. I kept working as best I could. It didn't become any better for me until I began to find my place with the others in the field. It didn't become easier because I learned to pick the melons, but because I learned to get along with the other workers.

It started by accident one day, while we were doing our melon-picking routine. We had a system. I picked the melons, tossed them up to the dark-skinned woman and she packed them into the crates on the truck. As I grabbed a melon and rhythmically swung it around for her to catch, that supposed-to-be firm melon liquefied into a massive missile of mush. She wasn't any faster than I was in sensing what had gone wrong; she grabbed at the melon which passed through her fingers and exploded into orange shrapnel all over her. I felt terrible — I didn't mean to do that. It was my fault. Up until then, we had never spoken to each other, even in an effort to be friendly — too cautious to try, because we probably both felt we were too different from each other. But that mushy melon seemed to suddenly break the barrier. We both looked at the sloppy mess we had made of ourselves and started laughing.

That evening, before I left for my motel room, I noticed her at the field washhouse. From another worker, I learned that her name was Juanita. She and her older brother had come north and left their children in Mexico – a hard decision brought on by a hard life. Whether Juanita ever had a husband, I never learned, but she had children to feed and no one else to earn money. In her destitution, this young mother left her children with her sister back in Mexico and came here to labor, picking crops as long as she could. Hearing that made me feel ashamed of my earlier feelings about her. Right then, she walked over to me and handed back the extra shirt I had loaned her. She smiled childishly and said,

"Me Juanita, you Pedro." My eyes opened wide and with schoolboy embarrassment I replied, "Well, I guess so."

"*Gracias, Pedro*, but do not squeeze the melons, please?" That was the second time we laughed together and it was not the last. Juanita and her brother began to change, or was it I who changed? They weren't any different after all. Her brother, Luciano, would interpret for her as she told me about her children in Mexico and how she missed her *angelitos*. Juanita was a loving mother — no different than my own mother had been, each picking her way through different fields in life.

Sometimes Juanita would invite me for a meal to their cabin down the row of little cabins near the fields. Theirs, like all the others, had a single light bulb hanging from the water-stained ceiling. Juanita had a thick spicy smelling soup ready as Luciano divided up the tortillas. I'll never forget suddenly looking up at a crucifix hanging on the wall. I immediately recognized the presence of my longtime friend in the room. It was a delicious and almost spiritual supper that we all shared with the Lord that night.

About two weeks later we were together again sharing a meal as we celebrated the end of the melon harvest. I felt that perhaps my Jesus was leading me into a new *familia;* a new direction in my life. Juanita, Luciano, and I talked and laughed well into the night. The world around us didn't matter. It was a joy to see Juanita's weathered face softened with a smile of simple innocence. She was a beautiful child in her own way. I thanked them each with a hug that night. I felt a real kinship with them.

The next morning when I got to the field, I saw two vehicles down the row at their cabin door. One was the foreman's pickup truck and the other was an official-looking van. They both drove away. As soon as I could, I hurried to Luciano to ask what had happened. "Where is Juanita? Are her children OK? Is Juanita all right? When will she be back?" Luciano looked at me. His eyes had turned thin and cold. He stared distantly at me as if he were struggling with words of anger. I felt confused and injured by his sudden change; I could sense a curtain falling between our eyes. *Why*, I wondered, was I being shunned? Was I too different after all? What happened to my friend Juanita? None of the answers came, other than Luciano's angered reply as he closed himself off behind the cabin door. "You *Gringos!* Because she had no card, you took her away."

"No, wait," I shouted, but he would not open the door. Shortly after that, the flatbed truck came and picked us up for work in a new field. I remember thinking about Juanita as we passed by the now-empty melon field. There was a little girl with dark hair along the dirt road waving her hand. As I passed her, she looked directly at me. I recognized something in her soft smile of innocence. I always think of that little girl disappearing into the dust as the last time I saw Juanita.

Feeling older, and perhaps a bit wiser that Fall, I made my way home from Colorado. As I drove those quiet hours back to my trailer in Farley, I began to realize something. Just like my want to return to Thailand to work in a leper colony years ago, now I was realizing that as willing as I would be to work with disadvantaged workers, it was not to be my calling. *Jesus, take me home. Help me find my way.*

I still wanted to help others less fortunate than I was. I became interested in the work of Mother Theresa's Brothers of the Poor in Los Angeles. They worked with homeless people on the inner-city streets. I had sold my trailer and property in Farley and had put my Jeep up on blocks at the Hefner's Ranch. With that and my savings, I headed to Los Angeles on a long, tiresome bus ride. Once I stepped off the bus, I sensed the difference from the quiet world I'd been living in for the past eight or nine years. Diesel fumes filled my nostrils and stung my eyes as I saw people laden with baggage, all in a hurry to escape the congested, noisy bus terminal. I made my way through the busy crowd and with travel bag held tight in hand, I leaned against the cold concrete wall of the terminal. *So many people!* I expected to see a van from the Mission House arriving to pick me up. To my surprise, a young man in ordinary street clothes and in sandals approached me, saying,

"You must be Pierre. I'm Brother Mark. If you'll follow me, we can easily walk from here. This is our neighborhood. We have some very dear brothers and sisters here on these streets that we help out daily." I pulled my attention away from the goings-on out on the street to say an exaggerated, "Oh."

"It is good, my brother Pierre, that you have come to us here." Hearing him refer to me as "Brother," made me feel good, even though I felt I hadn't done anything to deserve such recognition.

"Here we are," Brother Mark said, as he pushed open a large heavy iron door along the whitewashed, graffiti-marked wall. Once I stepped into the inner compound of the mission house, I immediately had a feeling of peace. I could sense an overwhelming presence of my Jesus, saying, *come in and help me.*

After a warm welcome by the Brothers, I settled into the modest accommodations at the mission house. I was given a pillow and a single blanket. I was told how all the brothers sleep on the floor in the common area. I looked around at the open room and placed my bag and sleeping gear along the wall. *Wow! This is really going to be down to earth.* I don't think I slept at all that first night.

The next day started with early prayers, after which I began to help with daily routines: going with my helper Brother down the alleys behind restaurants and asking for left-over food. Back at the mission house, we all helped the derelict souls from the street with food and shelter. After several days of the same routine, I began to feel confident in what I was doing. I enjoyed the challenges and felt blessed with the humility I could sense in myself as I helped others.

Ethel, an elderly woman, was one of my favorites. She was frail looking, with dark skin and red hair, but she was street-smart and tough. Ethel would come to the mission house several times a week. Because she always held her finger at her mouth to keep her upper plate from falling loose, I asked her, "What happened to your lower plate, dear?

"Only found one," she whispered in my ear. Each time she came to the mission house, she established her presence by saying, "Now listen here, White Boys, my name is Ethel and don't you forget it!" This seemed to be her way of maintaining her dignity in our presence, even though everyone knew her street name was Sip. I had seen her several mornings over in the city park, plying her charms before the men who were waiting for the washrooms to be unlocked.

"Hey, Sip," the men would jeer, "come on over here and I'll give you a sip of this," grabbing at their crotches. Ethel had her ways of earning a drink as well as her street name. Nonetheless, we would greet her kindly, dish out some warm food and give her a place to rest her frizzy-haired head for the night. Mother Theresa was asked how she could keep working with such destitute, needy people. She replied, "I try to see Christ in the face of each person, one person at a time."

Like all the Brothers, I had my place on the floor each night where I found rest with my pillow and blanket. Lying there, listening to the city sounds, thinking about Sip and the others I had met out there on the streets, I was beginning to see a little more clearly the real face of my long-time secret friend.

After some weeks, I began to sense problems, at least for me, in the way the Brothers' mission house worked. No one talked over difficulties they had encountered or even shared how to cope with daily stress. If they did, I wasn't included. No one cared about being trained in how to deal with gang members or with destitute street people who behaved erratically. Without any guidance, I became discouraged. Prayer is good, prayer is necessary, but daily prayers alone will not stop the knife in your back when someone on meth doesn't like waiting his turn in the meal line. In my opinion, we were lacking the special training needed to help a lot of others, as well as caring for ourselves. I had a great experience there with the Brothers; however, it wasn't the answer to my prayers. After a month, I decided to return to my New Mexico.

With no house in Farley or any place to live, I was grateful to accept the offer by my friends, Manuel and Mary Gonzalez, to live temporarily in one of the empty houses that they had on their large ranch. This humble little house was known as the Miera Ranch house. Remote and alone in this house, I enjoyed the peacefulness. I spent my days walking along the creek, riding horseback, or just enjoying the quiet of the valley. The closest person to where I was living was the postmaster at the tiny Bueyeros Post Office. It was no more than a small one room building, about half of a mile east of my house, close to the red buttes. Across the road from the post office stood the historic Sacred Heart Catholic church. When I would go to the post office every few days for mail and maybe a little conversation, I would often go over to the church to enjoy the comforting peace I felt there.

It was built in 1894 by a German missionary priest. It was the mother church for that whole part of the countryside, when New Mexico was not yet a state. The church was built in a traditional style with a steeple above the entrance. Inside the stone structure were three stained-glass windows along each side. They led one's eyes to the altar. Behind the beautifully curved wooden communion rail, the altar itself rose in layers of brightly colored columns and candlesticks. On the top tier and in the center of the wooden altar stood the almost life-size statue of Christ as the Sacred Heart, with his arms out-stretched. To both left and right of the statue of Christ winged angels completed the statuary. Behind all this on the tall back wall were the elaborate painted panels imitating stained-glass, thus expanding the visual experience to one of grandeur and beauty. They were a combination of gothic designs and Mexican folk art. Above the altar, near the peak of the ceiling, was a very large, round, clear glass window, the only window in the church that had no stained-glass in it. It looked like a gaping hole, compared to the colors below.

One day I was at the Bueyeros post office when Mrs. Libby, a local rancher, was there. She talked about the church and about how a few years ago, Father Sanchez, who was at that time their parish priest and not yet an archbishop, had helped them paint the church. He was now a local hero to the Catholic ranchers in the area. I'm sure all that praise was being repeated for my benefit. When the time seemed right, I asked her about the clear glass round window. She said she had lived in Bueyeros all her life, but no one could remember ever seeing stained glass in it.

One cold windy day when we were sitting around the warm wood stove in the post office, Mrs. Libby again told me about her childhood and about how the big clear window above the altar didn't have pretty glass in it. The outcome of that hour-long conversation was that she would pay me to make a stained-glass window to fit that space. *What a privilege,* I thought.

I had done some stained-glass work before, but nothing as important as this project. Mrs. Libby gave me some money to buy the necessary supplies for the window. Once the weather warmed up, I drove to Amarillo, Texas, for what I needed. I spent weeks at the Miera Ranch house meticulously cutting out glass and putting together all the leaded pieces for the approximately forty-inch diameter window. I chose a design with a bright red heart in the center, with radiating yellow and light orange rays, which spread outward to a double ring of sky-blue glass, which was punctuated with smaller red hearts. I was quite proud of myself for completing it. I didn't tell anyone at the time, but I scratched my name in the lead caning along the outer edge of the window.

Once the window was finished, Manuel came over from

the main ranch to help me raise it into place high over the altar. With no real scaffolding, we had to rely on several shaky ladders, all of different lengths. I was nervous as I climbed up past the plaster angels above the altar, while I shoved the heavy window up the ladder in front of me. I remember saying to myself, as if I were talking to the angels, "*So this is the way it looks from up here.*" Coming face to face with the Sacred Heart statue, I wasn't so smug!

Carefully we raised the round window to the waiting hole in the thick stone wall. It felt right, closing off the empty space. "*Please Corazon Santo, make it fit.*" It fit perfectly. Manuel climbed down his ladder while I was still up by the window. At that alone and quiet moment, I had the most wonderful experience. When the sunlight passed through the stained glass and painted its colors on my arms and face, I sensed an encounter with my life-long secret friend. It was so warm and peaceful in that very private moment. I didn't want to climb down, but stay there forever. It was both figuratively and literally the closest to heaven I had ever been in a church.

In the late afternoons at the Miera Ranch house, I always enjoyed the sun as it painted fire on the red rock butte immediately east of the house. One day, the view was different as a line of dust rose out of the distance from Bueyeros toward my house. Minutes later, a State Patrol car came to a dusty stop at the wooden gate out front. After the dust settled, an officer got out and adjusted his hat as he walked toward the gate. He must have located me through the little post office. We had no phones in this area, so he had driven sixty miles from Clayton to Bueyeros to speak with me. He told me that a Mrs. Reed in Albuquerque wanted me to call her about her son, Jim. That was it. I thanked the officer and he got back in the patrol car, turned around, and drove away leaving me with the dust and the worry of why Jim's mother wanted to talk to me.

Since the days when Jim was at the boys' ranch, I had occasionally gone to Albuquerque to talk with him to try to lift his spirits. It had been about a month since I had last seen him. Often, he would still want to kill himself. He was scheduled to go to Bernalillo Medical Center for another therapy session, but he didn't want to go. He said, when I was with him last month, that it was a waste of time — he would rather kill himself. He asked me if it would be OK if he did. He wanted me to give him my permission to kill himself — plain and straightforward as that. "The only one who cares about me is you, Pierre."

Suddenly I was back at the boys' ranch. He was having his diabetic crisis, he nearly died, I was next to him on the bed waiting for him to wake up, wanting him to get better. This time he didn't want to get better. He wanted to die. I could not convince him to live. With the prayer *"Get down here, God, and help me,"* I said to him, "Jim, I know you are tired of your life. Because you care for me, will you do something for me? I know you don't want to go back to BMC for more therapy, but will you do it this one last time for me? IF it does not work out, then you can kill yourself."

I felt an enormous weight when I said that. I felt that all the good I had tried to do would be nothing if God didn't help make this turn out okay. Jim thought for a moment, and said, "OK, I'll do it, but only for you, Pierre."

That was the way we parted that day, barely a month, ago. Now I was going to drive the sixty miles to Clayton the next day to find out what Mrs. Reed wanted to tell me. I had an ominous feeling about the call. *Was Jim behaving erratically, or was he in some kind of trouble?*

Morning started too early the next day. All the way, driving to town, I pondered about the call I was going to make once I got there. Arriving in Clayton, I went directly to the wall-mounted public phone outside on the grocery store and slipped my quarters in the slot, blung, blung, blung.

"Good morning, Mrs. Reed, it's me, Pierre." It didn't seem like the time for small talk, so I asked her what it was that she wanted to tell me. I could tell immediately by her voice that something was seriously wrong. Each word spoken came short of breath as she told me what had happened.

"Jim didn't stay long at BMC the way he promised you, Pierre." she said. "Then he started to do well for himself. He got a small apartment, then a job, all on his own. Things were going well. He was so proud of himself and anxious to tell you all about it, Pierre. He started a new job on Monday," Mrs. Reed continued. "Yesterday, Wednesday, I got a call from his employer who asked why Jim hadn't shown up for work."

When Mrs. Reed said the words, "I'm so sorry, Pierre," my heart sank. I sensed what was to follow. She continued to explain, "The police were notified and went to Jim's apartment. Anxious to get dressed on Monday for work, he passed out and fell. The lack of insulin probably caused him to faint. When he fell, he hit his head on the glass corner of the table and cut an artery in his neck. Jim bled to death."

I thought God was being cruel to me. Why was he taking back the only person who ever said that I cared for him? Jim was the one boy to whom I promised that I would always be there for him. Had I failed to do enough for him? This was my all-time low. I had lost too many people in my New Mexico life: my father to a grave in Tucson, Vaughn and Cecelia Marie to graves in the junipers, and now, Jim. What was left for me to do besides bury Jim? I felt that there was no one left for me to care about. No one.

I drove back to my house after that call, packed a bag, and started the long drive south to Albuquerque for Jim's burial. I got as far as Santa Rosa, where I had to pull off the road. I couldn't go any farther. I broke down in tears, crying my head off for several minutes before I could continue on. I owed it to Jim to be strong, so I tried.

By the time I got to the cemetery in Albuquerque, they were ready to lower the coffin in the grave. Jim's mother worshiped in the Bahia faith, so there was no embalming of the body — thus the need for an immediate burial. I was shocked when she asked if I would like to see Jim one last time. I hesitated momentarily, and finally said, "Yes." The funeral director reached over and raised up the top half-lid of the coffin for me to see. Jim's body was carefully wrapped in white sheeting with celestial symbols on it. His face was visible, but was pale blue. It wasn't the smiley, though sometimes bothered look of the Jim that I knew, but rather a distant-looking face of someone I loved, gone away. Goodbye, my brother. I asked Mrs. Reed if it would be OK if I laid a small cross on Jim's chest. She said, "That would be nice, please do." Before I left that day, I gave her the only picture I had of Jim. She was so grateful. It was the last thing I could do for Jim. I had the feeling that I was at the end of a road, still wondering, which road now?

LA BAJADA 9

O f all the different moves, I made, in efforts to find a new direction, this new feeling of unattachment had me totally confused. With Jim gone, the boys' ranch closed, and Father Ed moved away, I finally felt free of the last nine years. My obligations to others were over. Those were my reflections as I drove out of Albuquerque after Jim's funeral. It was late afternoon, and I was on my way back to the Miera Ranch house at Bueyeros.

I always enjoyed the drive north out of Albuquerque. The eroded red and tan hills along the interstate helped me imagine Spanish supply caravans with livestock and heavily burdened wagons toiling over rutted hills and arroyos as they spent days struggling to get to their Santa Fe outpost. La Bajada hill took me little more than three minutes to drive up, compared to the days it must have taken for past travelers. Overhead a hawk, guardian of the hills, circled effortlessly. His painted shadow crossed the road ahead, bumping its way across pottery-red clay ledges, only to be lost at the hill's high edge to the salmon pink color of the late afternoon sky. Miles ahead, the lights of Santa Fe came into view, glistening below the dark backdrop of the Sangre de Cristo mountains.

I pulled into the interstate rest area south of Santa Fe for the night. Sleeping in rest areas had become all too familiar to me over the past years. The routine was the same: drive past the washrooms, circle behind the building, and hope to find a quiet place to park for the night. It was already late in the evening, so I was glad to find an empty parking space away from the overhead security lights. I had to deal with the usual annoyances: the ever-changing procession of cars with doors slamming, dogs barking, children crying and the night long drumming of the diesel truck generators. I rolled over in my sleeping bag, wanting to sleep but unwilling to surrender my thoughts about Jim's burial earlier that day. What let sleep come at last? Perhaps the prayer, perhaps the "just let go" feeling, or perhaps simple exhaustion.

Morning woke me with a sore shoulder and the sound of a slammed side door on a van parked next to my truck. I had slept in my shirt and jeans, making it fairly easy to dress. However, I had to open the back of the camper to sit on the tail gate of the truck to put my boots on.

"Good morning to you," a man said as he hastily herded his kids past me. I didn't have time to respond. It dawned on me that this stranger was a person who didn't know me, who didn't know all the things I'd been through, and he was simply saying, "hello." This made me feel normal. It made me feel connected to people once again. Boots on, camper locked, I made my pilgrimage to the washroom and waited in line for my turn at a urinal. Men and boys flushed, washed, threw their used paper hand towels toward the already full waste container. Every one of us eager to get back to our interrupted journeys.

Driving north on Interstate 25 past Santa Fe and Las Vegas, I felt relaxed and at peace with myself. As I got closer to Wagon Mound on my way to Bueyeros, I couldn't keep from staring intently at the flat barren grassland to the west. Somewhere, out there, it happened. The images flashed in my mind of Phillip and Vaughn, out there in the grass, running away from the boys' ranch. Then I saw images of that cold night, wind blowing snow in the faces of two frightened boys as they tried to stumble their way in the dark out there in the prairie. I could see them falter, shiver, huddle in the snow. The frail, small, thirteen-year-old boy's face turning icy white. His sad eyes staring down from under lids crusted with snow. I could hear him hopelessly murmuring his last painful words to his companion, Phillip. "I can't go any more. I'm too cold. I just want to sleep."

"Here Vaughn. Take my extra coat. Sit here, Vaughn. Try to stay awake, Vaughn. I'll be back, Vaughn. I won't leave you, Vaughn. I'll come back with help, Vaughn. I promise."

How cruel the grasses were, mocking me for the life they had claimed. I sped on down the interstate, but I could not outrun the images of Phillip, trudging ahead, collapsing at some distant ranch house. I saw the dogs barking, emergency unit assist, lights searching blindly in the snow, but none able to help poor Phillip keep his promise to Vaughn. A double tragedy: one life lost and the other left to struggle with the memory of it all. I wiped away my tears and drove on, hoping to never pass that way again.

It felt good to be back in Bueyeros at my Miera Ranch house. But I felt different after so much had happened. I felt the need to do something for myself. I began to think that perhaps God was clearing the way for me to find a new life. Several days later, Manuel drove over in the morning from the main ranch. His faded green International pickup, complete with stock racks and a trailing of loose hay scraps, came to a halt in front of the Miera Ranch house.

"Hola, mi amigo!" he called out, as he indignantly spat

tobacco from the truck window in my direction. "You want maybe to go to Clayton with me? I'll buy lunch at Paloma Blanca Café. You come?"

"Sure, Manuel." I said, glad for the invite to be around people. The conversation was sparse as we drove to town. It had always been more of his wife's idea than his to let me stay at their Miera Ranch house. As much as I liked and respected Manuel, sometimes he treated me as if he had an ax to grind against all gringos for the way they had treated him in the past. I could tell he was now hinting that it might be time for me to move on. Halfway to town, Manuel surprised me with some new information.

"Oh, you know that Father Ed? He makes all kinds of troubles up in town at Roy and Mosquero. People don't like him, say he is a bad priest. Parents don't like him taking the altar boys on trips. Say their boys won't talk any more to them when they get back from one of Father Ed's trips".

"You mean Father Ed is the pastor at the Catholic church in Roy?" I asked.

"Si, everyone is afraid of him." I wanted to blurt out my whole story to Manuel, but knew it would do no good. It wasn't my fight anymore, but it did anger me to hear Father Ed was still on the loose. "That's too bad," was all I said, but inside I was seething with anger — no one yet had stopped Father Ed.

After we drove into Clayton by way of the feed store, I realized why he had asked me along. After loading twenty-four salt blocks, two new steel feed troughs and bags of pellets for his wife's chickens, I felt I earned my lunch. All the time we were eating, I thought about making a phone call to my brother in

Wyoming to see what he thought I should do. "Let's go," Manuel said as he flopped his napkin down on the café table. After his quick conversation in Spanish with the waitress, we were out the door with no time for my phone call. Back in his truck, we headed down the long gravel road back to Bueyeros. Mission accomplished for Manuel, but not for me.

GOODBYES 10

I was surprised to see Mrs. Libby drive up to the Miera house so early in the morning. I had just finished eating my cereal, so I quickly hid the bowl in the sink, wiped my mouth and headed out the door to greet her. I gave her a friendly wave of the hand as I slowly walked to the gate, allowing her ample time to get out of her pickup truck. It had been several weeks since I had last seen her. That was when she asked me to paint a picture of the Bueyeros church altar.

She was dressed in her usual outfit of blue jeans, Carhartt jacket over a western shirt, and baseball cap on top of a closely-cut head of white hair. Anyone else would have looked ordinary dressed like this, but Mrs. Libby, even in her senior years, had a high-class aura from her years as wife to the owner of one of the largest ranches in New Mexico. It was a challenge to please such a woman. She liked the stained-glass window I had made for the Bueyeros church; I had some hope she would approve the painting she was coming to pick up.

"Good morning to you, Mr. Peer Nichols," she said with chin slightly elevated. She knew darn well how to pronounce my name, but she liked to be condescending. I acknowledged her greeting with an up-tilt of my head.

"And a good morning to you, Mrs. Libby." Wasting no words or time, she headed past me, straight toward the house door, declaring, "Well, I've come to get my picture. You know how eager I am to see it." I smiled and with an eye roll followed her into the house. I knew she would be pleased with the painting because I had spent many hours on the details and finished it off with extra fancy matting. I offered her a chair at the kitchen table, hoping she wouldn't notice the dusting of sugar left from my hurried breakfast. She sat down slowly, tucking her arms under the table to hide an envelope in her hand. I could see her looking intently around the room as if to make up for all the years when she must have often wondered what it looked like inside this humble little ranch house. I didn't even have coffee to offer her at such short notice, so I said, "I've finished your painting, Mrs. Libby, and though it isn't perfect, I hope you will like it. I'll go get it for you."

I went in the other room where the picture was sitting next to the bed. When I peeked through the doorway, I saw that she was still looking intently around the room. She paused and stared at the cereal box I had left out by mistake. *Has she forgotten what a cereal box looks like?* She seemed to be deep in thought of it. When I deliberately kicked the door with my foot on the way out of the room, she snapped back and looked at me with her full attention. Out I came, walking ceremoniously into the room, carrying the large picture. Her smile of anticipation quickly turned to disgust as she saw I had turned the picture to show only the back of it.

"Now Peer. That is not funny. You better turn that picture around this very minute, you hear?" When I turned the picture around anticipating her approval, she looked close, staring at it as if frozen in place. Her face drooped into a look of pure sorrow. I was shocked. I thought she would like it. After a few moments of silence, I began to apologize saying, "I know it isn't perfect but I tried to . . . .."

"Shish!" she sternly demanded, while still looking at the painting. "Oh, Peer. Oh, dear Jesus! It is so beautiful!" She looked up at me with a big smile. Switching back into business mode, she produced the envelope from under the table and placed it on top as payment. I knew then that I had accomplished my task.

"I'll be getting on my way now, so you go put my picture in the truck for me. And see that you don't break it, understand?"

"Yes, Mrs. Libby."

When I came back in the house, she was still sitting in that wooden chair tapping her fingers on the table. She got up in front of me and stood there, arms straight down, looking at me. At first, I didn't understand what she was trying to say. Then I realized her difficulty. Her wealth and position made it difficult for her to simply say, "thank you" to a person like me. She didn't know at that moment how to do it. I slowly nodded with a smile; she did the same in return. That was all the "thank you" I needed. Underneath her crustiness, over time, I found a gentle, sensitive self — but only because she was willing to share it with me. I remember her with a special fondness.

With the last of several paintings now completed, I had enough money saved up to make a move from the Miera Ranch. First there were a few things I wanted to do. It had been over a year since I had last seen Father Jones in Springer — the priest who helped me on my trip to see the archbishop. I had heard that Father was coping with throat cancer. Remembering that he liked photography, I drove to Springer to give him all of my camera equipment. I wanted him to enjoy it as long as he could. When I presented it to him, he asked me, "Would you want it back later?" I almost burst out crying for him since I knew his cancer was terminal. I said, "Of course not. It's yours. One photographer to another." Saying goodbye to Father Jones was hard.

Next, I wanted to make that phone call to my brother. Taking another trip to Clayton, I pulled into the supermarket parking lot and waited my turn at the wall pay phone. My brother was living in Douglas, Wyoming, at that time and insisted that I move north. He was quite blunt. telling me, "It's about time you get your act together!" Those were hard but realistic words. They kept coming back and I felt restless all the following week at the Miera Ranch house. I was sitting in the very center of a teeter-totter, still not sure which side to lean to. Would it be Douglas, Wyoming — me with people, or Bueyeros, New Mexico — me the hermit? I recognized that I had been on a merry-go-round and it was time to reach from the horse and grab the brass ring. I had to decide.

I drove from my Miera house over to the main ranch house to tell Mary and Manuel about my planned move to Wyoming. When I told them, Manuel insisted on offering me a better car than my old worn-out Jeep. "This is the holy car," Manuel proudly proclaimed, "that once belonged to my very close friend, Father Sanchez, who is now the Archbishop of Santa Fe." *Not exactly my hero.* I did appreciate the exchange of vehicles even though the brakes on my new "holy car" didn't always work. I found that to be an ironic pay-back for what I had given the archbishop!

Before I packed my belongings in that faded blue 1965 Chevy Nova, I wanted to make one last climb to the top of Miera Butte. It is the tallest of three buttes in the Bueyeros area. Its straight vertical sides with layers of red, pink and tan sandstone made it look like a huge layer cake with a flat brown-rock cookie top. I had been up on top of it several times. The eroded, windblown soil still left up on top showed evidence of its early use by natives, either as a place of safety, or as a tool-working site. The trick to climbing it was finding the one and only way to the top. This time I was going to climb it to say goodbye to Bueyeros.

It takes a knowing eye to find the only place to start the climb. I found the faint trail at the base of the butte and followed it upward through the maze of tumbled stones and pieces of fallen rimrock I called "cookie rock." Next came the narrow passageway through the rock wall eighty feet above the ground. Like a short tunnel of some ten feet in length, it gave momentary refuge and a needed sense of security before continuing on the climb. The tunnel wall showed evidence of many hands which had passed through this womb toward the next stage of this rite of passage.

The easy part of my climb was over. Next came the narrow ledge exiting the tunnel way. Carefully, I placed each foot on the narrow walkway, forcing myself not to look down at the tiny mesquite bushes far below. I counted out every slow step until the seventh one got me past the ledge to a place of safety. Now that I was near the top, I had to face the final challenge. There, some eight to ten feet below the top of the butte, directly in front of my face was the precarious dreaded hanging ladder — an "Indiana Jones" challenge.

It had been years since I last climbed the butte. I thought the old wooden ladder would no longer be safe to use, but there

I was ready to risk it one last time. I could feel the wind pushing on my back as I gave a tug to steady the swinging ladder against the rock. *Please Jesus, hang onto the wire. Don't let it break!* Slowly, like a sloth, I raised myself cautiously up the rickety ladder one rung at a time. The third rung had fallen away, but the last two rungs at the top of the ladder were strong. Laughing at the devil wind and the somber grey sky, I pulled myself flat on my stomach, up onto that brown flat cookie rock and lay there for a minute to catch my breath.

I must have sat looking out at the grey gloomy openness of space for an hour, thinking about my past years in New Mexico. All the decisions, the trials, the sad, horrible memories came back — the boys' ranch, Father Ed, the deaths of Vaughn, Cecilia Marie and Jim. Everything was crying and screaming, spinning around in my head. *Leave me alone! I can't take it!* It was overwhelming. I felt a deep despair, one I had never felt before: an emptiness as if there was nothing left in me to live for. I wanted to end everything. At that dark moment, I stepped to the edge of that rock precipice, at the edge of nothingness, wanting it to be over. I looked down a hundred feet to the mesquite bushes waving their thorny arms, calling at me to jump. *"Give us your blood! Give us your blood!"* One more step, so close, but I couldn't do it. I failed through fear, too scared to die. Falling back, I crumpled down on my knees, trembling, as I thought of Jim. He wanted to die, but I saved him. When Jesus was on his mountain of temptation, he had angels to lift him to safety. Where were my angels, I cried? Where was my Jim to save me?

I remember those fearful moments of near tragedy and know that it was only my secret friend who pulled me back from the edge. I don't remember climbing down off the butte, only getting in my car afterwards and calmly driving the short distance back to the house, physically and emotionally drained. I lay in bed that night, thinking about my fearful experience on the butte. I never felt so alone in all my life, lying there in the silence. Only a prayer to Jesus gave me the hope for a better tomorrow.

Several days later, I went to say goodbye to my friends, Francis and Mary Hefner. They had moved to Clayton. Francis no longer did any dry farming; Mary was on oxygen, tethered to a long vinyl hose she dragged throughout the house. They had helped me over the years, helping to pay my expenses while I investigated the Hacienda boys' ranch, and welcoming me into their home when I needed a hug and a warm meal. They were able to leave behind most of those memories, although I couldn't. Like the Gonzales's in Bueyeros, the Hefner's were the last of my New Mexico family. Now I had to leave them behind too.

On the day that I left for Wyoming, I drove to the cemetery of Our Lady of Mount Carmel. There was one last thing I wanted to do at the graves of Vaughn and Cecelia Marie. I hadn't been back since Vaughn's funeral, now three years ago. When I got there, I opened the gate at the road and drove across the prairie grass to the little white church. Walking to the back of the cemetery, I found Vaughn's grave. The clumps of grass were easy to pull as I cleared his grave. Cecelia's grave was no longer cared for. The little stones around it that her siblings had carefully placed in a rectangle were now slumped out of place, victims of the harsh weather. The only identification for both graves were the little weathered aluminum markers left years ago by the funeral director.

It was late in the afternoon so I needed to get on with

what I wanted to do. Opening the trunk of my car, I took out the cardboard box that held three things which I brought to the graves. I had made two, eight-inch-tall, raw clay pots to leave at the graves for the elements to eventually claim — one for Vaughn, one for my godchild. Painted white, they each had words written around the rims. Cecelia's pot read, "Promise when we meet again, you'll remember me." I picked some nearby wild flowers and put them inside the pot and placed it on her grave. On the cleared spot on Vaughn's grave, I placed his bowl with an arrowhead in it. Around the rim the words read, "Fear not Vaughn. There are no fences in Heaven."

After a prayer, I reached in the box and took out the third item. Grasping the cold hard steel of the wire cutter in my hand, I went to the fence posts and snipped the barbed wire strands that separated Vaughn's grave from the rest of the cemetery. I rolled up the cut wire and threw it in the trunk of the car. *There. I did it.* I couldn't help turning around to face the junipers and the sky, and in raven's ear I yelled out loud as I could, "No more fences Vaughn. You are free!"

I heard my words echo as the sun set low behind the dark juniper hills. Everything was eerily silent. One last look. One last sadness. I drove away.

SOMEWHERE WYOMING 11

There was no going back. I had said goodbye to New Mexico and was on my way to, Some Place, Wyoming. My blue car, the one I called my "holy car" because it had belonged to the Archbishop of Santa Fe, was loaded with the last of my earthly possessions. Before I left the dirt road north of the cemetery, I stopped only long enough to open the car trunk and throw that jumble of barbed wire from the cemetery fence into a dry arroyo. After that I was ready to go.

Since I no longer had a camper to sleep in, I decided to splurge on a room at a motel in Raton. It was an April evening as I pulled into the Motel 6 parking area. *Check your wallet. Make sure you have enough money. OK, now go get a room.* Ahead of me was a young couple with two little boys, was signing in at the office. I was glad to wait my turn. One of the little boys was nagging his mother while the other was hanging onto his father's pant leg. All four, looked weary from travelling. I tried not to stare. *What if someone saw me looking at those boys? What if they thought I was like Father Ed?* I had programed myself to try to think like him, to get inside his head, to walk in his shoes. I knew I would have to work hard to get out of those shoes and to get his thoughts out of my head. I had to reclaim my healthy self.

"Oh, I'm sorry. Just tired from driving. Yes, sir, I'd like a room. Yes, just myself."

"Will you be staying longer than one night? The clerk asked.

"No, I'll be leaving for Wyoming tomorrow."

"I guess you like wind and snow, do yeah?" Giving an indignant raise of my chin, I replied, "It isn't that bad." But I really knew nothing about Wyoming. I was exhausted that night; I slumped into bed, trusting in my prayers that I would be kept safe on my long trip north.

That next morning, I was up early due to the usual door-slamming down from my room; people were eager to be on their way. After making sure I wasn't leaving anything in the room, I checked out of the motel and drove to a convenience store to get some travel snacks before I left town. On the main street, I passed by Salono's boot store where the ranch boys used to get their first pair of boots. I gave a slight goodbye wave in the direction of the store and continued out of town.

The route north out of New Mexico into Colorado on Interstate 25 goes over the high Raton Pass. I remembered it from ten years ago, when I was coming down into New Mexico on a bus. Now I was going to be going up the pass in my "holy car," hoping there was more to its holiness than just the name. I could feel the car straining to make the long grade up the pass as if something behind was trying to magnetically pull me back into New Mexico, calling, *"Come back. I'm not done with you!"* Once I topped the summit of the pass and was headed down-hill into Colorado, I finally began to feel everything was going to be fine. *Please God, make the brakes work!* I thought about my old friend Jesus who was with me and I was comforted.

As I drove through towns on the way to Wyoming, I was a little fearful because it might be difficult for me to re-enter society after living so long in little, remote Bueyeros. My mind occupied the miles thinking about all I probably missed out on in the past few years. Thinking about how to act, how to look, or even how to talk to people made me apprehensive.

Soon there would be no more miles to worry me. The next day, tired and feeling relieved, I turned off the interstate at Douglas, Wyoming. The exit ramp quickly became the main shopping area as I drove past a car dealership, a grocery store, a Village Inn restaurant and, of course, a KFC — iconic symbol of every successful small town. After southern Wyoming's treeless plains, it was pleasant to see a town with shade trees along the streets and well-kept lawns.

Several blocks further, I caught sight of a sign, "St. James Catholic Church." Curiosity made me turn the wheel as I made a quick right turn, following the arrow. One block ahead on the corner of a quiet residential street was the church. Sitting close to the corner sidewalk, the light-red-brick structure rose high above the encroaching trees into a classic bell tower complete with conical spire that held high a metal cross.

It was an impressive little brick church, although it showed its age. The grounds around the building were dry grass and bushes that had grown too large over the years. The concrete walkway between the street curb and the two steps into the church was broken into a mixed hop-scotch of pieces, the cracks invaded by rows and clumps of unwanted grass. The solid dark-green double doors at the center were weathered and drab in contrast to the stained-glass windows to the left and the right, each begging for more light from behind the imprisoning wire mesh that covered them. St. James Parish Church reminded me of Corazon Sancto Church in Bueyeros — both grand old buildings worn out by time.

While sitting there in my car, parked across from the church, I took a moment to relax and say a thank you to my Jesus for my safe trip to Douglas. I had the thought, *I'm going to go look inside the church.* No one was around so I slipped out of my car, cut across the street, and walked up to the front doors. The old pipe handrail was shaky. While looking down along the cracked concrete steps, I noticed a wine bottle half hidden in the bush. The bottle cap was screwed on it. Odd that I noticed that. It brought back a memory of an elderly gentleman I helped while I was doing mission work on the streets of Los Angeles. He had suffered a stroke, and yet he was surviving by shuffling between mission houses for the help he depended upon. I could hear him telling me again, in his slurred words, his story about wine bottles.

"You shee dar two kinds of drinkers. You gots da ones dat day jus drinks ta get drunked. Day trow the cap away inda street, den do their drink'n, then trow the empty bottle in da park. They not serious ones. We know we drinks fir the medicine in it. When ya see a bottle stand'n up with da cap on it, you know we respected da spirits inside." Here was a bottle standing up in the bush outside of St. James Church. I wondered if the old man's story was true everywhere and if so, where was the bottle's owner?

Focusing on the dark-green wooden church doors, I yanked hard on the right-side handle, pulled the sagging door open, and filled the church interior with the echoing sound of old wood grinding across the concrete threshold. No one was inside, only the bright light coming from the stained-glass windows on each side above the altar. The interior floor, pews and side walls were of dark wood while the upper walls around the side windows were painted white. The curved white ceiling was accented with graceful wood arches supported by fancy carved corbels — an expensive interior for its day. Straight ahead, my eyes led me directly to the large familiar statue next to the altar. There, almost smiling at me, was the same Sacred Heart of Jesus statue that I came face to face with in the Bueyeros church. It was as if my Jesus had arrived just before I did, to stretch his arms out once again to let me know that he was still a part of my journey. I walked up toward the front, genuflected, and moved sideways into a pew to say a prayer and enjoy a moment of peace. I heard the swish of the door opening behind me and closing again — but no foot steps up the wooden floor, no sound of anyone entering. Time for me to leave.

Back in my car, I couldn't help feeling a connection to this little church of St. James. Barely an hour had passed since I arrived in Douglas and already I had the feeling of belonging. I needed to find my brother's house, but I felt sure I would be back on Sunday for mass at this church.

Living temporarily with relatives is never comfortable for long. The welcome I got was real, but so were the inconveniences of my living with my brother and his family. Although my brother did his best to welcome me and to help with my transition, I knew I needed to find my own place.

Sunday came and I was eager to go to mass at St. James. When I arrived well before the start of mass, I parked down 5th Street to observe people as they arrived. It surprised me to see so many cars and trucks parking along the streets. I followed into church behind a group of people who were patiently squeezing through the front door. All the pews in the back were full, so I had to go all the way up front to find a place to sit down. It made me feel very self-conscious; I felt that everyone was looking at me. Soon mass started with a piano-accompanied hymn. Then the priest entered from the side sacristy followed by two altar boys, both of whom were taller than he was.

I wasn't paying much attention during mass. Father gave a good sermon and tried his best to befriend everyone. Looking around at folks, especially when they came forward at communion time, I could tell they were upset with the priest. I thought, *Oh no! Another bossy arrogant priest like Father Ed? I hope not.*

Mass was over. Faint words of the closing song quickly gave way to the sounds of parents with children all clambering to get out. I genuflected before the smoldering candles and the brass crucifix on the altar, and followed down the aisle behind the last of the parishioners.

"Good morning......Good morning" Father offered to each one on their way out, only to receive little response.

"Good morning to you, Father." I said with a smile. He was surprised. His serious face softened with delight.

"And, how are you? I don't believe I've seen you here before. Are you travelling through town?" I again felt self-conscious about my transient look of faded denim jacket and worn out Salano boots.

"My name is Pierre Nichols, Father, and I'm going to be moving here. I'm from New Mexico."

"I'm Father Phil, welcome to Douglas and St. James."

"This is quite an interesting little church you have here, Father Phil."

"You have no idea. I was assigned to this parish a few months ago. So far, they haven't hung me! I'm the lucky priest who had to come here to tell them that their beloved old church building was crumbling into ruin, and that I was here to tear it down and build a new one."

"Not too popular, huh? I said.

"It's the shits! Bishop Hart said, go and do it." I was taken back by the way he talked, but I could understand his predicament. Trying to put some salve on the wound, I said, "Well, Father, I suppose the bishop sent you here because he knew you were the best one to rebuild this parish." Father shrugged it off with a flip of the hand while mumbling something in Italian.

He obviously didn't want to offer details, so I was about to step away when he asked, "Had any breakfast yet?" Without time for me to rely, he said, "You come with me. We'll go to Village Inn. My treat. Jesus said, feed the hungry and I'm hungry and so are you." Nodding his head as if answering for me, he asked. "Is that your Chevy Nova over there?"

"Yes." I could tell he seemed amused looking at my pale blue car complete with dry mud splashing's in the wheel wells. Shaking his head, he said, "You better ride with me." I thought, *if you only knew who else once sat in MY holy car!"* I followed Father across the corner to his little silver Honda. It was the first time I had ridden in a completely functioning car since that trip from Springer to Albuquerque with Father Jones. I felt good riding with Father Phil. I had met a friendly priest and was on my way to a free breakfast. Not a bad start. When we got to the Village Inn restaurant both the hostess and the waitress were friendly to Father Phil and made sure he was comfortable in what seemed to be his usual booth next to the windows.

"Now let's see what should we get. Pick anything you want, Pierre." That's what I did: scrambled eggs, bacon, hot coffee and even pancakes. Everything was good, including our conversation. I quickly saw Father Phil's real friendliness and sincerity. While his Italian temper might have been a bit abrasive, his genuine down-to-earth caring about people and issues came through. He talked about how he had specialized in journalism at the diocesan communications office in Cheyenne, where he was the editor of the state Catholic newspaper. I also shared about my work at the boys' ranch in New Mexico; however, I steered away from the troublesome parts. Father said that the little house across from the church was the rectory. The upstairs of the house was rented to a man working at the uranium mine.

"With the big boom in uranium going on all around here," Father explained, "it's hard for workers to find places to rent. He's a nice man; however, he handles what they call Yellow Cake. You know, the hot stuff. He refuses to take his required work shower at the end of his shift. He comes home, contaminating the whole house. It's a wonder the whole damn place doesn't glow by now! He'll be leaving at the end of the month. After that I'll ask the ladies to come and clean the house extra good before I let the apartment out again."

"I'm staying at my brother's house here in Douglas until I find my own place. Tuesday, I'm going to drive to Ohio for my niece's wedding. I have a special song I want to sing for her with my guitar." Hearing that, Father said, "If you play a guitar, we could use you here at St. James." Trying not to commit to it, I nodded thoughtfully. As friendly as Father was, I wasn't about to jump into anything quite yet — lesson learned (I hoped) from the past. Once back from breakfast I thanked Father again and said, "I'll be away in Ohio, but I will be back before the end of the month and perhaps see you again."

"Anytime, Pierre. You're welcome at St James."

"Thank you, Father Phil."

ON THE ROAD AGAIN 12

*B*LAM! *Oh God, please help.... shoulder pain....my head hurts.... hang on!* That's all I remember until I woke up in the ditch, staring at my dirt-splattered windshield.

"Hey man, you all right?" a blurry face at the side window of the car asked me. I tried to focus while I asked myself the same question. I had dozed off on my way to Ohio, driven off the edge of the road, and caused a twisting series of death-defying skids with the G-force equal to a space launch. Luckily, *or was it my co-pilot,* I was able to keep the car upright until it hit the bottom of the ditch.

"Yeah, I think I am." I answered back.

"Yo Bro! Come on. This dude's stuck."

"Cool man," the other black guy said as he jumped out of their car and came down from the road toward me. *Oh no! I'm about to get mugged.*

"Get out of the car," one said in a low voice. What else could I do? They had me and my stuff. I sat in the grass, watching helplessly as one of them got behind the wheel and the other stood in front of the car, ready to push. Never had I imagined that my little blue car could squeal as much as it did when the guy revved the engine. With mud and grass flying everywhere, he popped that car back up onto the side of the road, ready for their taking. *What am I going to do now? Hitchhike to Ohio with nothing?*

"Here you go man," he said as he handed me the keys. I must have looked like a grateful puppy as I stared in his face. These two weren't thieves. They were two black men I had so wrongly profiled. I felt ashamed, knowing that my unwarranted fear probably showed. I had thought I was understanding and accepting; I wasn't. I bowed my head, acknowledging my mistake in judgement. His face never softened as if to say, *See, this is who we really are!* "Thank you so much," I said, as I reached out and shook his hand.

After that brief touch from the hand of Jesus, they got back in their fancy car, turned up the music, and sped away. I brushed the dirt off the windshield of my car, climbed inside, and looked around to see if everything was OK. My guitar wasn't damaged; my clothes were messed up, but the car was fine. Down near my foot I found my magnetic statue and put it back on the dash. As if nothing had happened, I headed down the road, singing prayerfully, "*I don't care if it rains or freezes, as long as I got my plastic Jesus, riding on the dashboard of my car.*"

That happened on my second day of driving. The following day, I drove into Youngstown, Ohio, and arrived at my sister's house. Everyone was excited as they prepared for my niece's wedding. We were all glad to see one other, but it felt distant. My life had been different from theirs. We found it hard to find anything to talk about. The next day was the wedding; the weather was beautiful as was the whole ceremony. Both my niece and her new husband were pleased with the song I sang for them. At the reception, I tried to keep my conversation limited to what it was like in New Mexico, being careful not to get into details about the disastrous boys' ranch. I wasn't ready to talk about it.

"Oh, that sounds very interesting. What are you going to do now?" I was asked repeatedly. It made me feel defensive; I was vulnerable to criticism because I didn't have a good answer.

With one day remaining before I left for Wyoming, I decided to drive to Mercer, Pennsylvania. I wanted to see the lake property that I had sold several years ago to help pay my expenses while I was in New Mexico. The property was in what was then a newly-developing community centered around a small lake, Lake Latonka. The plot I owned was only a grassy hill side, edged with a few small trees that I planted back in 1968. Now there was a stately two-story brick house on the property, complete with a grand driveway and beautifully manicured landscaping. Down at the lake, the wooden, narrow dock where I used to tie up my sailboat had been replaced with a fancy metal dock harboring several in-board pleasure boats.

Revisiting old places, reliving the past, wasn't the best use of my time. I toyed with the thoughts, *should I have stayed here instead of going to New Mexico? What if David had never called me to go? What if Jesus hadn't become my friend, leading me toward volunteer work?* I mulled over this in my mind, but I was at peace because I wasn't the only one making decisions for my life. My journey to the Hacienda de los Muchachos Boys Ranch in New Mexico was the path God had directed me onto — a mission that had to be, a mission more important than anything else I might have done. I was satisfied. Yes, I had gotten a few offers that would have brought me back to Ohio, but I liked my life out West, finding my own way, and trying to follow the whispers of my special friend Jesus, as he led me down my own path toward new discoveries. After that week, I said my thanks and goodbyes and hit the road once again, heading to Wyoming.

The scenery is good on a cross-country drive, but even better is the time it provides for in-depth thinking. I remember juggling ideas in my head: anticipating my return to my brother's house in Wyoming, and thinking about how he would help me. *That interesting priest Father Phil might be a good person to get to know well.* I looked forward to both brother and priest, and to returning to mass at St. James Church. Yes, I felt good. My Jesus was still with me stuck *"on the dashboard of my car."*

BIG PLANS 13

The long two-week round trip to Ohio was over; I was glad to return to Douglas, Wyoming, late in the summer of 1980. Seeing the town appear like a green furry patch surrounded by tan hills of grass reminded me of how I first saw Farley, New Mexico. The big difference was that this new island, Douglas, was prosperous. *No lazy dogs sleeping on these streets.* Douglas was going to be my new hacienda with a bright future for me.

"Well, how did the wedding go?" my brother asked. We sat around the dinner table that night as I shared the details as best as I could.

"As you see by the boxes, we're moving." With that, he looked blankly at me as if giving me time for the implication to sink in.

"Oh, cool." I replied. "Where are you heading?"

"Got another position open near Casper. Same outfit. Going to have to be there in two weeks, so." I knew what he was saying with that, "so...."

"I have a lead on a temporary place I can stay, no problem. The priest at the church here rents the upstairs apartment in his rectory. He said it was available now." I was bluffing, since I really didn't know that yet, but I had to say something.

"There you go again!" my brother said with a look of disgust. "When you going to learn, Pierre?" His reaction reminded me of how distant we had become over the years, and not only because of the miles separating us; the unfortunate effect of different influences in our lives. I had only a few days to find my own place; I wanted to sit in the little brick church one more time before I crossed the street to talk to Father Phil about the apartment.

When I turned the corner, heading for the church, I was shocked by what I saw, or didn't see. *What happened?* There was no church! The trees were there, but the church was gone. It was as if my Jesus wasn't going to let me have one more moment of pretending I was in my safe place, as if I was back in the church at Bueyeros. I parked once again in front of the parish center and looked across to where the church had stood. All that was left of it was a rubble-filled hole with some pipes and wires sticking out of it. The cracked sidewalk was gone, but, for some strange reason, the two concrete steps at the front of the church were still there. *Step right up folks! Church is open!* This was too fast of a change for me, so I drove down to the Covered Wagon Drive Through to get a satisfying chocolate shake.

While parked there, I looked at my little plastic statue of Jesus and thought for a moment, *Time for me to get busy, Jesus.* I put him in the glove box for safekeeping. Mustering up my courage, I drove back to the rectory. Actually the rectory was only an old Victorian house that the parish used as a rectory. I pressed on the round door bell and heard it ringing inside.

"Well, hello, traveler!" came from behind the door even before it was fully open. I was glad to see a welcoming face from the Father Phil I remembered. He said, "Come on in and have a seat. Don't worry, you won't light up," referring to the uranium man who rented from him before. "The ladies cleaned up everything after he left."

"Oh, good!" I felt that I had gotten to first base. The apartment was empty. "What happened to the church, Father?"

"Too bad you weren't here to see it. We sold off the stained-glass windows and some of the other things that were inside. The pews and altar pieces went to another church in the diocese. Then the demolition crew came. They knocked down most of the building with a bulldozer; they tied a big cable around the standing steeple and pulled on it with the dozer. Finally, it weakened and came crashing down in the middle of the street."

"What did the parishioners think?" I asked.

"Well, what could they say? It had to be done. I let them take away all the bricks they wanted. Kind of sad to see, but I think they are coming around now and making it a little easier for me, knowing it had to be done."

"Has the bishop come up from Cheyenne to talk to the parish about the change?"

"Of course not. I'm on my own. We have mass now over in the basement of the parish learning center. That's the building where you seem to like parking that pretty blue car of yours." We both got a good laughed out of that one.

Having satisfied my curiosity about the church building, Father elaborated on the plans for the new church. It is interesting how things work out. By the end of the afternoon he had implied that they would eventually need a full-time custodian for the new church as well as for the other two buildings, the parish learning center and the rectory. He said that his extra apartment was empty. That's what I was hoping to hear. He might have been in the glove box, but my Jesus was still answering my needs. Three days later, I moved temporarily into the upstairs apartment in the rectory. There wasn't anything Father Phil could hire me to do at the moment; however, he talked to a parishioner who arranged a part-time job for me with the local plumber.

Gene had the family plumbing business and was not only my boss, but also a good friend. He liked to razz me about my left-handed way of picking up a wrench. Eventually I remembered to put the wrench on the correct side of the pipe. I even learned how to sweat copper fittings. Once I had a little money saved up, I moved from the rectory apartment to across the street into a basement apartment that was owned by the Bowmen's. They lived on the one intersection corner that the parish didn't own.

Fred and Tessie Bowmen were an elderly couple who once had a ranch north of town. Sorry to say, but she was a bossy, loud person, while Fred had the gift of poor hearing, but also had poor memory. All the neighbors knew and loved Fred. Often, he would wander down the street and go into someone else's house, thinking it was his. Tessie told me, "Fred never was a good business rancher."

"How come?" I replied, hoping not to fuel the flames.

"I told him, and told him, don't you sell our sheep ranch! He wouldn't listen to me, not Fred! Sold off the whole place along with the mineral rights. All I got out of it was this house in town and baa, baa, baa!" I had to hold back from laughing at her interpretation of a sheep. Poor Tessie couldn't let go of her anger.

One day, when I finally decided to sell my worn out "holy car," Tessie eagerly offered me Fred's red 1964 Falcon. It had a permanent place in the garage where Fred spent time sitting in it, probably to get away from Tessie. "He doesn't need to be sitting out there in that dirty old car, hiding money in it from me." Tessie said. I found a buyer for my blue Nova that I had driven from New Mexico, and bought Fred's Falcon from Tessie. Obviously, he had no say in that decision.

Once it was mine, I drove the Falcon around to the back alley of the rectory where Tessie couldn't see what I was doing. After I gave it a thorough cleaning, I searched to see if there was any truth in her claims of hidden money. Sure enough, I found seventy-five dollars rolled up under the dash. It was Fred's get-away money. Tessie was pleased when I returned it to her. The Falcon was a good car. I even took it elk hunting that Fall. I'm sure it would have been a sight, if I had hauled home an elk on top of a red Falcon. Unfortunately, I wasn't lucky at the hunt.

All the while, the new church was taking shape across the street. Old Mr. Scott from 6th street would pass by in the evening to check on the progress. He was a staunch Methodist, and skeptical of the shape of the new church, comparing it to his church over on 4th street. Our new St. James church was designed to be heat efficient, with a low ceiling and a large graceful roof rising to a modest cross on top. The building was octagonal rather than rectangular. Mr. Scott would say, "It doesn't look much like our church. I guess you won't have any corners inside for the devil to hide in, hah? Looks like a Pizza Hut to me."

"Well, it isn't, Mr. Scott. It's the BIG Catholic Church." *So there!* He had been in the war, had a bit of a limp, and lived by himself. I let him talk; I knew he had no one else to talk to. Several years later, after I became the full-time custodian at

St. James, the VA hospital in Cheyenne dropped Mr. Scott while moving him into a bed. This left him paralyzed and unable ever again to return to Douglas. I went to see him one time. He asked how things were, and whether his house was still there. I thought that was a strange question to ask.

"Then I want to sell it. I'm never going back, you know. Would you like to buy it?" he asked. "I don't care what you want to give the bank for it. Just have them keep my military uniform in a box for me until I die." He had no relatives left. It struck me to think, *is this what it all comes down to when you are left alone in life?*

About a month later, I returned to Cheyenne with the papers for Mr. Scott to sign. "Now are you sure the bank has my uniform, so I can be buried in it?" he asked, panting with an oxygen tube in his nose. I assured him that everything was in order. He rested his head deeper into the pillow with a satisfied look on his face. He reminded me so much of my grandfather on his death bed, who also smiled when he knew that everything was taken care of.

I bought the house from Mr. Scott at a bargain price, and I was grateful for the opportunity to have my own home. It was a small stucco house with an old horse barn, on the other side of the block behind St. James Church. I never heard what happened to Mr. Scott, but I remembered him in my Catholic prayers. Soon after I was settled in my house, the transmission in the Falcon started going out. I traded it towards a new 1980 Datsun truck. Life was good to me, and so was my Jesus.

Father Phil and I got along very well. The parishioners also experienced the loving, spiritual leadership of Father, and the parish prospered. One day I was talking about New Mexico with Father Phil. I went into some details about how Vaughn had died back in 1976. While I was describing Vaughn's grave, Father looked sad. Hearing the story, he asked, "What do you think about putting a real tombstone on Vaughn's grave, Pierre?" I couldn't speak. The lump in my throat was too much, choking off the words my mind was trying to put together for me. All the sleeping tears awoke and welled up behind my eyes. Trying my best to hide them, I replied, "Father, Vaughn was left there, his story untold, his family somewhere far away. I think about the silent hills that hold him, and the raven, his only friend there, calling him each day to say, "*I haven't forgotten you. I see where you are.*" It's a vision I see over and over. It really would be nice if Vaughn had a proper tombstone so someone would know exactly where he was. Certainly, he deserves that."

"Well then, let me have the correct information and we'll get it done, Pierre."

"But, Father, it would be too expensive, wouldn't it?"

"Never mind. I can get a good price for the stone, and you can pay me back whenever you can. Then you go down and put it on Vaughn's grave." With that agreed, I felt grateful to Father and excited to be able to do something that would honor Vaughn forever. He would not be forgotten.

It was over a month before the freight company delivered the stone. When it came to my house, I called Father. I put the crate on the tailgate of my truck and drove to the rectory to show it to him. He was standing at the curb looking excited, with a hammer in one hand and a small bottle of holy water in the other. I had the thought, *if they ever make a saint statue of Father Phil, that's the way it should look. Hammer and holy water, would say it all!*

When we opened the crate, I was speechless, seeing how beautiful the approximately two-foot by one-foot stone was. The grey granite and black high-lighting of the carved words were elegant. It definitely was first class. Father was pleased too. Without saying anything, he uncapped the bottle, and, while sprinkling some water on the stone, blessed it. It touched my heart that Father Phil cared so much to be a part of my journey. I couldn't wait until warmer weather when I could take a trip back to New Mexico to place the stone on Vaughn's grave. After so much time away from there, I could sense some trepidation about going back, but like a moth drawn to a flame, I knew I couldn't stay away, especially with this special mission for Vaughn. That was the first time ever that I wanted to return.

MY MISSION 14

During the early 1980's, while working for the parish of St. James, I became involved in a unique relationship. Not the usual one between man and woman, but one with a special type of loving. It was as if Jesus was giving me the opportunity to risk loving once again after so many losses. I embraced my new love and welcomed him into my home and my heart. It took some time before Charlie and I got used to each other, but our love was unquestionable. Parishioners could see us walking together, and knew it was the best thing for me even if they didn't all care for my choice, meaning, his type. I loved Charlie's eyes, his touch, his willingness to forgive and accept me for who I was. He was my love of life, my gift from Jesus, more than just a big hairy, Irish Wolfhound.

Springtime finally arrived blown in by the usual Wyoming wind. For weeks, I had been spending my time preparing my truck for the trip back to New Mexico. Charlie would be going with me on this trip; I had to arrange the camper shell on the truck so he would have his own space for travelling. I built a raised plywood bed along the left side of the truck bed for me to sleep on. Under it was space for packing things I needed to bring on the trip, such as shovel, cement, extra clothes, and Charlie's things. On the right side, I carefully boxed in the rest of my stuff, leaving room for the crated tombstone, as well as for Charlie. The day finally came to leave for New Mexico. Father Phil came over to say goodbye and to see me off on the trip. I had purposely not loaded the crate myself so he could be a part of it. When he got to the garage, we lifted it almost ceremoniously into its designated place in the truck.

"You have all the tools you need?" he asked.

"Yes, Father."

"You have enough gas? Do you have enough money? Don't forget to call from time to

time so I know you are alright."

"Yes, Father, I'll be OK, see?" as I pointed to my plastic Jesus. He laughed a little though his concerns were obvious. Charlie jumped in the back of the truck and I closed the tailgate, ready to go.

"Don't forget...."

"Father, I'll be fine. Thank you again for everything." He gave me a hug and a blessing before I left that morning.

Driving out of town, I felt proud of myself. I had a home, a parish family and a place I would be happy to return to. Once again, my Jesus was with me leading me on. Charlie poked his big head through the double sliding back windows into the cab next to my shoulder as if to say *"Let's go!"* Buckle your seat belt and hang on Charlie. We're headed for New Mexico!"

It felt good driving down the interstate once again. Three years in Wyoming had passed quickly, and I felt a strong desire to return to New Mexico, not only to place the grave stone on Vaughn's grave, but also to see the changes and to realize that I too had changed. *Would I ever be able to forget the boys' ranch? Can the heart heal without scars? Might I find some answers on this trip?* Time and the miles would tell.

After two days of driving and surviving the traffic south through Colorado, my trusty Datsun truck crested the top of Raton Pass at the border of New Mexico. I was excited, looking down in the distance, seeing the familiar dark green hills, volcanic cones and mesas, all resting like islands on the unending see of tan grasslands. I felt I was home. When I got to Raton that night, I went to the Motel 6 the same as I had done years ago. I remembered the comments that the desk clerk had made about Wyoming, so I had planned on showing off my Wyoming driver's license to let him know I survived and was doing well in Wyoming. When I got to the motel office, I was disappointed to see a different clerk. It was a reminder to me that things were not the same as before. That night, Charlie, my trusted friend and companion, slept in the back of the truck by himself.

There were a number of things I wanted to see on that trip. Of course, the main purpose was to place the stone on Vaughn's grave. After that, I wanted to see what was left of the Hacienda de los Muchachos ranch building. That night it felt good to rest in a real bed after bunking with Charlie in the back of a cramped truck. I was close to all the things I wanted to see and do; I had trouble settling my mind and sleeping that night.

I woke up the next morning before first light of day. I packed out of the room as quietly as I could and checked out at the office desk. Charlie was ready for a walk and chow. I went to a gas station, got gas, grabbed a pre-wrapped sandwich and a cup of coffee. I felt eager and excited as I headed out of town toward Clayton.

The road east follows along the bottom of the high basalt-rimmed Johnson Mesa to the north. I reminisced as I drove, remembering places along the way where I use to arrowhead hunt and hike. The early morning sun peeked through the film of low clouds ahead and fired its orange color over the whole mesa, blanketing it in Spanish gold. I was taken with the sunrise view of the mesa and missed my turn off. I had to turn around and go back to find the gravel road south that I wanted. This backroad led to Farley and passed by Our Lady of Mount Carmel cemetery with its little white church.

As I drove down the gravel road, the trailing dust cloud behind the truck seemed to give away my impending arrival. Everything looked the same as before, but I couldn't help feeling out of place, like an alien visitor, no longer the local I had once been. Topping the last rise in the roadway, I could see off to the right in the distance the dark green hills as they slowly surrendered a view of the little white church. It looked so alone and forgotten. *Don't feel sad. Do what you have come to do.*

Driving up to the fence gate, I saw that the nearby ranch house had been closed for a long time. I saw no evidence that anyone was around, even though I had the feeling that eyes were watching me. Perhaps they were the raven's watching and wondering from the junipers why I was there. Crossing through that bumpy, rutted pasture, I headed toward the back-corner fence of the cemetery. I noticed that the fence had been moved further back and that now Vaughn's grave was officially within the cemetery instead of outside of it. Perhaps the clay pot I left on his grave with the words of shame got the job done. By now, Vaughn's grave had a blanket of grass over it, giving it a warm, peaceful look. I cleared the space at the top of his grave for the stone and took out all the equipment I had brought with me.

My shovel scratched its way into the quiet soil down through chips of stone and dirt as I dug out the rectangular hole that would hold the wooden frame for the foundation. While scooping out the last loose dirt with my hand, I stopped frozen in place as I felt I was back here again on the day of his burial. I could picture the people around me, sense my heart painfully beating and feel the crush of soil in my hand. It took me a moment to come back to the present. As I set aside the soil, I remembered those words whispered to me. "Just let go. Just let go."

Once the hole was dug, I set the frame into it. Using the water, I had brought, I mixed cement and filled the box, leveling it off with a carpenter's level. I felt a sense of pride in doing with dignity what Vaughn deserved, something that needed to be done. While setting the stone permanently into the cement, I couldn't help smiling and mumbling words of comfort to Vaughn as I finished up the work. It looked proper and peaceful. I thanked God for the opportunity He gave me to live beyond that rocky precipice of despair I had faced at the Bueyeros Miera Butte. I had lived long enough to bring honor to Vaughn's grave. Nearby was the lonely grave of my godchild, Cecilia Marie. Nothing had been done to give her a proper marker or stone. I was sad, thinking that none of her family had ever come back. I promised I would never forget her as I reset new stones around her grave.

But my job wasn't done yet. Now came the part I didn't tell anyone about, not even Father Phil. Before I left Douglas, I wrote a letter explaining everything that I knew had happened at the boys' ranch, all about Father Ed, and particularly about Vaughn's death and about his brother Alan. I put the letter in a sealed Mason jar and brought it with me. Now, with the stone in place, I took my shovel to the cemetery's large wooden cross. In a hidden place, I buried the jar. *There, someday you can tell the story if it is still unknown.* After that I didn't want to stay any longer. The morning breeze felt cold and unfriendly. No raven's call could be heard overhead. It was as if their guarding task was over.

Back at the truck Charlie was waiting patiently. While loading up the shovel and other equipment, a thought came to me. *What else could I give to Vaughn?* I walked back through the graveyard past forgotten gravestones, retracing the funeral's steps up to Vaughn's grave. I knelt next to it. On top of his beautiful gravestone, I left my plastic Jesus.

That evening back at the motel, I called Father Phil to let him know that the mission had been accomplished. I also told him that I planned to see the old ranch building where everything had happened.

"Are you sure? Will you be all right?" he asked with concern.

"Don't worry, Father. It's something I have to do."

The next day, I re-packed the truck and headed south on interstate 25. When I reached Springer, New Mexico, I took the state road east toward Farley, where the boys ranch had been. *What will I find?* I drove into the little town with much anticipation. The old front street looked eerily the same, except there were no people. Not even a dog for Charlie to bark at. No one anywhere. When I first saw the old adobe school building, once home of the Hacienda de los Muchachos Boys Ranch, my mind flashed back, recalling the fun times with the boys, the times playing in the snow, and the mud puddle fights in the summer.

But things had changed; I saw the hollow windows that showed blue sky behind them. The elm trees, now dead, stood naked along the front of the building, while swallows circled, protecting their coveted nests above the open entrance way. Hoping not to find the ghost of Father Ed within, I ventured to enter that abandoned shell of a building.

The crackle of fallen plaster under my feet announced my return as I stepped cautiously from the lobby toward the boys' hallway. I had the strange feeling that, somehow, I would hear boys' voices calling and talking together as in years gone by, but no sounds were there as I moved through the entrance way. The steel double doors that once held back secrets were gone. Peering down the long hallway where the boys' rooms had been, I felt I was looking into the ruins of Pompeii. There no longer was a ceiling or a roof over the building. The inner adobe- plaster walls still showed patches of animal designs that the boys painted years ago, but now all was collapsing, filling the hall with debris. The blue sky directly above took away the darkness of the place, and I was glad for that. Suddenly I turned and saw it. There, broken down, lying against the wall, half covered in adobe and plaster rubble, was Father Ed's blue door. The blue door of evil. Anger burned in my mind as I grabbed at the trash and at the heavy stucco sheet that had fallen against it, so I could kick the devil out of that door. But I looked at it again and sensed sadness. The old door was weathered from exposure, the color fading away. Cracked and peeling, blue paint was falling in chips like autumn leaves, only to be lost in the adobe dirt that had entombed the door itself. I backed away as if hearing a voice telling me *"do not touch!"* I had seen enough, so I solemnly left the building, leaving the elements to finish their task.

Across the road where I use to live after I left Father Ed and the boys' ranch, my old trailer had been moved away and the property left vacant, the same fate of the few other houses that had once been holdouts of aging residents. I was satisfied to have seen what I had seen. I drove out of Farley with a heavy heart, not wanting to look back and glad to be on my way, Silver City was my next destination.

I had heard about that town where there were cliff caves or dwellings down in that area. Sounded interesting. It was a long drive south through the traffic of Santa Fe, Albuquerque, and further on to Deming, New Mexico. From there I had to drive north passing Cook's Peak, to get to Silver City.

On the way, I pulled into a state park called City of Rocks. Not exactly the city I was looking for, but at least it was a place to rest for the night. At that time, it was undeveloped, and seemed to be a strange place in the dusk of the day. The rounded giant boulders stood close together, hiding a maze of shadowy pathways. I pulled my truck up next to a huge odd-looking boulder and joined in the quiet of the place. I spent the night with Charlie next to me. Both of us got little sleep. All during the night, I couldn't help looking out the window, watching moon shadows moving among the boulders. I was sure there were spirits moving around in that spooky light.

Charlie wasn't the only one tired of all the miles. *Just a little more Charlie and we'll be in Silver City.* Driving into town, I was surprised to be in Juniper-and pine-covered hills. It was a refreshing change from the flat desert lands I had driven through the day before. I was also surprised to see so much development. My mind was still stuck on visions of Farley and other small towns I had seen along the way. Silver City had a university, lots of businesses, even a KFC. I was quite impressed. I got mixed up driving around the historic part of town. I kept going in circles before I figured how to get back on the road south out of town.

Before I left, I stopped to eat at the KFC. While waiting for my box of chicken, the woman waiting on me asked where I was from? I wondered, *how did she know? Was it my cowboy hat that gave it away?* I told her a bit about my journey and she was interested and friendly. It made me feel, Silver City was a welcoming town.

I was now at the end of the sixth day of my journey. In the next three days, I would drive straight back to Wyoming, back-tracking all the way, same gas stops, same rest areas and same fast food. It was a tiresome drive, and poor Charlie was as exhausted as I was. Along the way, I thought about what I had seen and concluded that I had found answers to my heart's questions.

Would I ever leave behind my thoughts about the boys' ranch? No, it will always be a part of my heart, both pain and joy together. Will it scar my heart? Yes, but not enough to keep me from loving. Feeling satisfied, I drove on. No plastic Jesus to look at, but I knew he was with me. Charlie poked his head through the double sliding back window of the cab. "Home's just a little further down the road, Charlie. Let's go."

THE VISITORS 15

Somewhere deep in my subconscious I must early on have connected success in life with priests. Maybe it was the influence that my mother's cousin, Father Mathieu, had on me. Perhaps that connection was my motivation for working with Father Ed at the boys' ranch, even though that didn't work out. I never realized a true, spiritual, working relationship with him. Now, working as the custodian at the Catholic church in Douglas, Wyoming, I found fulfillment working alongside a truly spiritual priest, Father Philip Colibraro.

Besides my working hours caring for the church properties, I became involved in playing in the music group, in planning special liturgies and church decorations, as well as designing the stained-glass windows for the new church. Father Phil was innovative, and the people of the parish grew spiritually under his creative guidance. I enjoyed working for him and thanked God for finally giving me the chance to experience an honorable priest. I had my home, my hobbies such as hunting and camping, and my friendships with people outside the parish. I had a happy life and a priest who helped heal my broken faith. That healed faith, that feeling of belonging to the church, was to be tested one spring morning some six or seven years later.

Father Phil had been re-assigned to Our Lady of Fatima parish in Casper, Wyoming. St. James parish in Douglas was now under a new priest with a new parish council, which wanted to gain full control, now that Father Phil was no longer on the scene. One Monday morning in spring, a car pulled up in front of my house just before it was time for me to walk over to church and start work. As I went out to see who it was, I recognized my plumber friend Gene and some members of the parish council. Since no one seemed to want to get out of the car, I leaned over to talk to Gene as he sat by the car window.

"Good morning, Gene," I said, with a smile. Neither Gene nor the others in the car said a word in response. Something serious was about to happen; I could tell by the look on Gene's face.

"Pierre, we are here to tell you that you no longer have your job with the parish." It took me a few seconds to comprehend what I had just heard. I was dumbfounded.

"Why don't I have my job? Did I do something wrong, Gene?" His eyes were downcast; he didn't want to look at me.

"Where is Father to tell me this?" I asked.

"Father left yesterday on a retreat out of state. The parish council with his approval has eliminated your position."

"But you still will need a custodian, won't you?"

"It was a financial decision," one of the men cowering in the back seat said.

Sensing the meaning of all this, I replied, "I would be willing to work only part time if that would help?"

Gene cleared his throat and raised his head to look me in the eyes.

"I have to ask you to give us your key to the church, now.

Your pay check will be sent to you in the mail, after Father returns."

"Could I volunteer to help?"

"No. That won't be necessary."

Finally, I saw what they were doing. I was eliminated once Father Phil was away and the parish council could control the new priest. They finally re-gained their control of the parish. My working friendship with Father Phil was probably one of the reasons for my being fired. It had nothing to do with finances. When I returned from the house with the church key, I also had a pair of pliers in my hand. The people in the car didn't care how I felt or had any concern for me at all. I was about to let them know just what I thought of their cowardly business.

"This," I said to Gene and the others in the car, "is what you have done to me." I used the pliers to break the key in half. "Here you are." Gene looked stunned as I put the broken pieces of key in his hand. He stared at me momentarily as if sad for something, perhaps for the fading away of our friendship. He nodded to the driver, and they drove away. How cruel they were to treat me that way.

To my knowledge, nothing was ever said to the parish about all I had done over the years. No thank you from anyone; I was just fired. When the new priest returned from his alleged retreat back East, he called me to the rectory. He looked nervous as he presented an envelope to me containing five hundred dollars of his own money. He offered it, he said, "to help me out." I looked at the envelope of guilt money and said, "Is this a scorpion or an egg in your hand? Either way, I will not take your payment." With that I left and never talked to him again. I was bitter. It was a lousy way to be treated. I could imagine my Jesus was also upset.

After that morning, I had a difficult time calming down enough to call Father Phil and tell him what had happened. He was surprisingly calm and consoling, telling me to just move on, forget the wrong, and look beyond it. But that was hard to do. Could I go to mass at St. James again? I needed a job. I had truck payments and a loan on my house. *Maybe I should have stayed in New Mexico.* It took some time for me to quell my anger and disappointment in everyone, even in my Jesus for leading me into that bad situation.

Finally, I decided to sell my house and move away from what St. James had now become to me. It hurt too much to look out the kitchen window across the alley to the church. Nothing good was left for me in Douglas. My faithful wolfhound Charlie was gone; his absence was another reason to move on to a better place. Father Phil continued to be a good friend, helping me as I wobbled between different ideas of what to do. I thought about returning to New Mexico, but I knew that would be like running away from making a better decision.

The sale of my Douglas house went fast, and I was pleased to realize a very good profit from it, something, I felt sure, Jesus had arranged. After searching around Casper, Wyoming, I found ten acres in the country just west of the city; it wasn't listed for sale but I heard that the realtor who owned it would be willing to sell.

It was a beautiful spot with a high ridge from which the views of the mountain nearby were spectacular. After I purchased the property in 1990, it was like, Homesteading 101. I dug fence holes, strung wire and hauled rocks and dirt, all before I had a modest house built on the top of the ridge. After the second year, I was able to have a Western Art gallery built down the hill by the road. Besides my own art work of small sculptures, paintings and gourd art, I had other artists represented in my gallery. I was the proud owner of "Goose Egg Gallery," on Goose Egg Road, west of Casper, Wyoming. I was in business and earning my keep — blessings I'm sure my Jesus had given me.

I became involved at Our Lady of Fatima Catholic church in Casper. When it came time for a major renovation of the church, I was given the honor of designing the new entrance vestibule, as well as the huge stained-glass front windows that stretched from floor to ceiling in the entrance way. This was a much larger project than the stained-glass windows I had designed back in Douglas for St. James church, or the round window for Sacred Heart church in Bueyeros. I was proud of all I had accomplished and enjoyed my life. Jesus and I were back together, just like before.

For over five years, I was successful in helping out in my new Casper parish. My mountain home and gallery were my delight, even though the surrounding property owners were jealous that I had purchased the property they all hoped to get. Nevertheless, I continued to build up my business and my life. I had come a long way in the fifteen years since New Mexico.

One day in 1995, while doing my artwork at the gallery, I got an unexpected phone call. Ms. Billie Surnum was calling from Albuquerque, asking if she could come to Casper and talk with me. She wanted to ask me some questions about the Hacienda de los Muchachos Boys Ranch. I immediately felt protective, even defensive, not knowing what direction she was coming from. She told me that she was a private investigator representing two young men who had been at the ranch. That eased my concerns, but I was still cautious about committing to anything with her.

"Why would you want to talk to me?" I asked. "That was so many years ago."

"I would like to ask you what you knew about the ranch and Father Ed's behavior." My mind pounced like a wild tiger at the thought of all I could say to her. It was as if all the thoughts and images from the past were in a thick book and my mind's thumb was rapidly fanning through the pages, seeing everything flashing by in a split second.

"Well, Ms. Surnum, I doubt there is anything I could be a help with." All the while I knew differently. "But if you want to come here, it would be OK with me." We agreed on a date in the following week. I was to meet her at the Casper airport on the following Thursday evening.

All that week, I pondered over what she might ask, and how I could answer it, rehearsing the scenarios over and over in my mind. There was the matter of my documentation and materials from the time of the ranch. Several times in the past years, I had seriously considered destroying all my boys' ranch journals and documentation — all those details of interviews, carbon copies of letters to the archbishop, everything. But I never did. Perhaps this meeting was the reason I didn't. I still had all the important papers sealed in a big manila envelope. What would happen, I wondered, when I meet with Ms. Surnum? What would she ask?

What would happen if I allow her to lift the lid on Pandora's Box and see all my records?

A Private Investigator sounded intimidating — possibly someone working for a money-hungry lawyer. I wasn't going to tell any high-class investigator anything important. I didn't trust anyone to know everything. *Why should I be involved now; after all, the boys have all moved on in their lives, Father Ed is gone, so why now, Jesus?*

Casper airport was empty the evening that I went to meet Ms. Billie Surnum. The last flight for the night had arrived, and almost everyone who had arrived on it had left the airport and were on their way home. The long corridor, lined with airline counters now closed, was a tunnel of silence, quiet in the absence of anyone coming or going. Down at the far end near the luggage area, I noticed a woman in blue jeans and long grey hair, standing against the wall with a knapsack over her shoulder. She was eating a sandwich from her oversized shoulder bag. I couldn't help thinking, she looked like a left-over hippie, fallen there from some old, dysfunctional time machine. *Could this be Ms.Billie Surnume? No, this one's no lawyer!*

"Excuse me," came a call from behind me. When I turned around, I saw a pleasant-looking woman smiling at me. As I was about to say, "Hello, Ms. Surnum," she asked, "Have you seen a tall man with a little girl here? I'm waiting for my husband and daughter. They are on their way to pick me up." Looking surprised, I replied, "No, I'm sorry, I haven't." I came close to embarrassing myself.

By now the only two people left in the area were the woman

with the knapsack, and me. That woman was now coming up the corridor toward me.

"Hello," she said, as she came over to where I was sitting. "You have to be Pierre. I'm Billie." Her long silvery, straight hair fell like open stage curtains around her face as she leaned forward, extending her hand toward me. Wrinkles crossed her face like roads on a map, showing lines of experience. I stood up quickly and took her warm hand in mine. I had the feeling that this gentle woman might soon be drawing new lines on the map of my face.

"Yes, it's me, Pierre, and I'm pleased to meet you too." I said. As I walked with her to wait for a taxi to take her to her motel, I couldn't help laughing at myself for thinking harshly of her earlier. This person I had just met was warm and friendly, not arrogant or impersonal at all. *A private investigator with long hair and a knapsack? This should be interesting.*

The next day she called early from her motel to arrange a meeting. I thought about a restaurant meeting place, but decided to invite her to the house where it would be casual and private. Her cab dropped her off on the road at my driveway next to the gallery. I watched from the house as she adjusted her briefcase and handbag, and began the climb up the driveway to the house.

She had a pleasant way about her as she meandered forward, spinning around at times to take in the view and all I had done to the property. Her obvious appreciation impressed me. Once we were comfortably sitting in the kitchen, we enjoyed coffee and the sweet rolls she had brought with her. I felt very comfortable talking with her and could sense she was genuinely looking out for the two boys she said she was representing.

That afternoon and all the following two days, we talked about many things. Slowly, we both were peeling back the years and uncovering the details of life at the boys' ranch. I could tell she was patiently leading me into revealing the facts she had come to hear. I knew she was drawing me out, but it didn't bother me since I could tell her heart was in the right place.

After the second day, I finally shared the contents of my manila envelope that was bulging with all my journals and papers. I watched silently as she reviewed the various documents — the boys' testimonies and the carbon copies of letters that I had sent to the archbishop and other officials. I could tell she was deeply disturbed by it all.

There were times in our conversation when she would ask something about me as if to verify what she may have already heard from someone else. Perhaps she was checking me out as well as well as learning new facts about the ranch. Throughout our talks, she recorded much of what I said. It was painful for me to talk about my frustration over the cover-up at the ranch. After periods of serious talk, we took breaks and shared things about ourselves. Billie understood my pain from losing those whom I loved. She told me how she had gotten back from Hawaii recently, where she buried her only son who had died from AIDS.

As much as I would have liked to know which boys she was representing, I never asked her. Could it have been Jessie, who saw his father get shot, and who slept curled up in a ball every night? Or Ron, who was serving time in the correctional facility in Las Lunas, New Mexico. Or Kenneth, who was dropped off at the ranch by a parent who had kept him on dope when he was a little child? I wondered, but I was afraid to know more, because I didn't want to get sucked into the vortex of pain again. I willingly gave Billie all the help and information I could, and she made copies of much of my material. Perhaps more was happening that she didn't tell me about. Whatever it would lead to or put in motion, I didn't care. Someone needed to know the facts.

When I drove Billie Surnum to the airport for her return trip to Albuquerque, I was satisfied that she was doing something for the boys. That made the stress of the last few days' worth it. It still seemed strange to me that she had found me in Casper. Was I still unknowingly involved? I could only wonder what else my Jesus had up his sleeve.

Driving home from the airport, I felt relieved. Pandora's Box had been opened successfully after so many years. I knew I would never know everything that my meeting with Billie had set in motion, but it didn't matter. In the back of my closet, under my old Solano boots, I put away that heavy manila envelope one more time.

TWO STEPS FORWARD 16

Nothing could be crueler than to have to endure the aroma of sizzling fried chicken and not being able to taste it! I had to face that torture every Wednesday evening while I sat in my gallery across the road from the "Goose Egg Inn," just west of Casper, Wyoming. I could endure the aroma of burgers and steaks drifting across the road from the restaurant, but that tempting smell of fried chicken was often my downfall. Almost every Wednesday evening, after I was finished at the gallery, I would walk over to the Inn to satisfy my hunger for Irene's special pan-fried chicken.

The restaurant itself was not impressive on the outside. The front of the building was covered in blue-painted barn wood boards with only an entrance door and no windows. Once inside, the atmosphere was a welcoming mix of antiques, an old western style bar, old leather booths and linen-draped dining tables in the main dining area. The interior was dimly lit and a little spooky, mostly because of the stuffed game animals peering down from the paneled walls.

I was told some thought the building was haunted. Irene's staff refused to be in the building unless she was there. Perhaps it was the ghost of Alberto hanging around in the cellar.

According to one version of the story, years ago, in the 1930s, the original Goose Egg Inn was a small wooden building across the road from the present-day brick building. An old sheepherder would frequent the Inn several times each year. His usual drink during those prohibition days was corn whiskey supplied by two bootlegging brothers in Casper. Alberto's taste for the distilled elixir of corn mash was only a little stronger than his second love, homemade pie, especially peach pie. Each year in August when peaches were in season, the cook would bake her peach pies at the old Goose Egg Inn. 'Seems it never failed that the old sheep herder always managed to sneak in the kitchen and steal off to the cellar below, with one of those peach pies all for himself.

Whether he was down there in that cellar the evening in August 1934 when the old wooden inn caught fire and burned to the ground, no one knew for sure, but he was never seen again. As the story went, even after fifty years and after the inn was rebuilt, on a still night in August one can sometimes smell the faint aroma of peach pie coming up from the storeroom below at the Goose Egg Inn. I never did smell any peach pie drifting in the night air to confirm the story, but I certainly remember that pan-fried chicken!

The area of Goose Egg was an inspiration to many local artists around Casper. The name "Goose Egg" came from the historic Goose Egg Ranch that was described in the novel, *The Virginian*, by Owen Wister. In the novel, a scene was set in 1882 at the Goose Egg Ranch mansion, where a diner party was being held. Some of the men were upset with the hostess, so they sneaked upstairs where the babies of the parents were sleeping. They switched the babies around in their covered cribs. When the tired parents took up their sleeping babies and returned to their homes after the evening event, they were horrified to find that under the wrappings were different babies from their own. This account in *The Virginian* keeps the story of the Goose Egg Ranch alive although the old stone mansion no longer exists.

Over the next few years, I forgot much about my past and lay aside thoughts of the boys' ranch. I produced numerous small ink drawings and paintings of the Goose Egg Ranch house, as well as other collectable pieces related to the local history. Besides my own art work, I had over a dozen artists represented in my gallery. As time moved on, so too did some of the artists, as well as some neighbors in the area. The cranky doctor and his wife down the road, who seemed intent on making my life miserable, succumbed to old age. They had been jealous of my gallery and my accomplishments. Some locals led by them tried to have my gallery closed on the grounds that the colors of the gallery trim were too green, the lights were on too long at night, and my fence was in the wrong place! Despite the occasional harassment, I was determined to survive.

But just surviving isn't all there is in life. I learned that years ago, when I decided to move to Wyoming instead of staying like a recluse, in New Mexico. As much as I loved my home and property, I wasn't at peace in Casper. After six years, I felt I had accomplished all that I wanted to. I had built my house and the gallery and landscaped the property into a picture of beauty surpassing anything in the area. I was proud of it all. After my accomplishments, I felt it was time for me to listen to my inner callings. Those were the callings to go home. Home to New Mexico.

It took several months before my Goose Egg property finally sold. During that time, I made a trip to New Mexico, searching for a new home. I could not resist the lure of going through Farley on the way south to relive old times at the boys' ranch. It had been fifteen years since I was last there. All the while driving south, I wondered what I would find.

When I turned off the interstate and headed east out of Springer, the prairie that had impressed me the first time I saw it back in 1969 still looked timeless. The occasional ranch houses along the way showed some changes, as children grew up and took over from their parents. The memorable Pepto-Bismol-pink ranch house was now empty and dull. Perhaps it was waiting for a new generation to come and restore it to its former glory. When I got to the turn-off for Farley, I noticed that there was no longer a road sign for "Farley." *Had the town disappeared? Had it finally lost its past?* On the drive toward the town center, huge new pylons shadowed the road to my left. Their high voltage cables cast gracefully curved shadows on the road ahead, tempting me to drive along those curves.

At Farley, I found nothing that I hadn't seen before. The same old buildings didn't bring back any fond memories. I looked at the remains of the old school building that was once the boys' ranch. Just as the echoes of high school events had passed away, so too the short life of the boys' ranch and the echoes of the boys and Father Ed were finally gone from the site. I sensed it and was happy to finally close the book and to leave behind a place I once knew. A place that wasn't there anymore.

That first trip south from Wyoming was mainly to explore New Mexico. I wanted to see different towns to decide where I might want to live. It wasn't until the second trip that I finally found my new place. Although it wasn't the easiest town to get to, as it wasn't near an interstate, I found myself in Silver City once again.

"There is this really nice place out in the country, Pierre, that I think you will like. It's in the Mimbres Valley, east of town," my realtor, Carol, said.

"Well, let's go see it. I wouldn't mind living in the country again," I said with enthusiasm. When she took me to see the place, I wasn't sure what to think. The property was a jungle of overgrown sumac trees and shrubs, all crowding around old tired-looking outbuildings and sheds. Rusted chicken wire hung like sagging lace curtains from one shed, signaling a chicken coop. At the front of the property, hidden behind a half-dead apple tree, was a small stucco house with the rusty corrugated roof typical of old houses in New Mexico. Beneath the side wall of the house was a weathered door to an old root cellar.

Brushing aside the hanging vines on a sagging wood trellis, I made my way onto the cobblestone porch so I could look inside the house. Peering through the wrinkly glass window in the door, I could see chalk white walls in the small room. They were streaked with trails of brown adobe washed down by past rains that had leaked through from the roof. Well-worn floorboards led my eyes to a lone chair in the corner. On a side wall, a bird had made a nest in the open end of a stovepipe hole in the wall, left over from a long-departed kitchen wood stove. Another room, no larger than the first, was built onto the end of the front room. Beyond that, another, and another, each with a ceiling a bit lower than the one before. As empty as it was, I could still sense a lingering warmth from the family that had once lived here beckoning to me.

Outside, warm sunlight-lit rocks lined garden paths, which were barely visible through the fallen branches and waist-high weeds. Nearby, tangled in a tree, stood a windmill with missing blades. It looked toothless and cried in rhythmic squeaks, "*Here I am. Listen to me.*" All this ruin spoke of someone who had once loved his little patch of heaven. I could see myself restoring the buildings and bringing it all back to life. I could clear the weeds, plant new fruit trees. I could bring back life to the sleeping little homestead. Reality clicked in. I knew I would be starting another "Homesteading 101." I hadn't chosen to move to New Mexico to spend my retirement years doing that again.

"I have the contract here, Pierre. All you have to do is sign it," Carol said as she hastily opened up her folder on the hood of her car. It was tempting, but I declined. A day before I was to return to Wyoming, I found a house in Silver City. The purchase took some time to finalize, and I had to make another trip between Wyoming and New Mexico, but I felt blessed to finally make the move to Silver City. *Thank you, Jesus.*

The house I bought was a true adobe needing repair. The exterior stucco walls were cracked and gave hordes of wasps easy access to the adobe blocks inside, where they no doubt were happy to have a home of their own. After the first monsoon rain, I noticed how badly the roof leaked. There was much to fix up, but it was my new house, my home to be. One of my first projects inside the house was to build into an adobe wall a *nicho*, where I could keep my Jesus. This was an antique crucifix that Father Phil had given me years ago in Wyoming. I wanted the crucifix to be in my hallway where I would pass by it during the day, to remind me of the many journeys the two of us had been on, and how blessed I now was to be happy in Silver City.

Retirement for me still included some of my old interests. The area around Silver City, with the Gila National Forest outside the back door, offered endless opportunities for exploration. Soon I became involved in the local archeology group and developed an ongoing interest in doing gourd work in the style of the ancient Mimbres culture, which was found in the area east of Silver City. Years before, when I had my gallery in Wyoming, I had become interested in gourds as art pieces. Gourds are the natural shape of primitive vessels. Mimbres pottery inspired me to create gourd art based on their black-on-white style of painting. This pursuit of gourd art led to openings for me in various galleries, as well as to juried shows in the surrounding states.

I now had to learn to use a computer. Reluctant as I was, I had to accept a changing world. The computer was the way to go even though it confused me. I have a brain for art, not for mechanics or electronics.

On an ordinary afternoon in December of 2011, when I was on the computer, out of curiosity I typed in my name to see if anything would come up. When it did, up popped the devil! Or was it an angel? What I was reading shocked me. My name came up in a document, a case study by the Crossland Foundation based in Baltimore, Maryland. The foundation, headed by Dr. Leon J. Podles, researches and exposes the truth about pedophiles among Catholic priests. I was unnerved by what I read in the study of Father Edward Donelan. The whole story, and all the facts about him and the ill-fated Hacienda de los Muchachos Boys Ranch, were now a matter of public record.

In the case study, I read how I had been credited with "being the only one who had the decency to stop it." I nearly fell out of my chair. I could hardly comprehend what had happened over the years, and what it now meant. I could now read about my efforts to help resolve the situation with Father Ed Donelan and the Hacienda Boys' Ranch. I realized that all the records and the carbon copies of letters that I had allowed Ms. Billie Surnum to take with her back in 1995 were probably part of this documented case study. I hope all that information helped to bring about a settlement on behalf of the boys whom she represented.

Indeed, much had happened that I was unaware of. All those years since I buried that secret jar near the cross in the cemetery of Our Lady of Mount Carmel, I thought that I had to bear that burden of knowledge all by myself. Now I knew that for me the burden was gone. I was finally free of it. Others knew the truth. I never wanted any acknowledgement for doing the right thing, but there it was, and I thanked God to live to see the day when the facts were known to everyone. I knew my Jesus was smiling down at me, probably saying something like, *"See Pierre, how things are working out?"* I cried tears of relief.

I wrote to Dr. Podles and told him my story about the ranch and about Vaughn, the boy who froze to death. He was quite moved to hear about Vaughn and my personal journey. I thanked him and the Crossland Foundation for the investigative work they were doing. I felt strengthened. The truth was out there, and my involvement now made me feel proud of myself in a way I hadn't felt before.

It is hard to explain how things come together. Why was it there in Silver City, sitting at a computer, that I would feel the connection to the boys' ranch was coming back? It was not a revival of past feelings, but a feeling of something new happening, a sensation of moving forward. This became even more obvious when the strangest thing of all happened next. Out of nowhere, several months after the revelation from the Crossland Foundation, I received a phone call.

"Hello, I'm calling from California. I found your name on the internet. Are you the Pierre Nichols that use to work at a boys' ranch with Father Ed, years ago?"

"Yes," I replied. At that moment, I felt a shiver of fear, wondering if this was trouble coming my way. "And you are?" I asked.

"This is Tomás. Do you remember me from the ranch?"

"Oh, Tomás! Of course I do. What a wonderful surprise! I've thought of you often, wondering how you were."

"Well, I'm doing really fine. 'Got married years ago and have four great kids. I even took them to New Mexico to see the old ranch where I grew up."

"That's great!" I exclaimed.

"I guess I want you to know, Pierre, that I'm fine and hope you are too." We talked a while about life since the days at the ranch, sharing memories of the past, but we left out any sad or troubling times.

"I never had many photos of you guys at the ranch, Tomás, but one of the few that I do have is a small wallet-size picture that you gave me from school. I've kept it all these years. If you send me your address, I'd be happy to mail it to you. I bet your boys would like to see it. I'll email you this afternoon."

"It would be nice to see that picture again."

"I always remember your smile, Tomás, and I am glad you called. Take care, my new-found little brother." As soon as I hung up the phone, I thought my head would bump on the ceiling. I was so excited, I had a hard time coming down from it. To think that I would hear from one of the boys was astonishing to me! That next day I followed through with my email and waited for his return letter with his address, so I could respond and send him the picture. It was a good re-connect, hearing from one of the boys. Enough for me to feel pleased that I could now close the book on the boys' ranch.

But the book just wouldn't close. Soon after hearing from Tomas, I got an email about another boy who had been at the boys' ranch. *What's going on?* It was the Crossland Foundation once again, asking if I cared to correspond with a man who was looking for me; he remembered me from the old boys' ranch. I was so excited that I quickly emailed back, "Of course!" But I was suspicious. Not of the boy, but rather my old friend Jesus. *Just what do you have planned for me now?* I didn't know it then, but in that year of 2013 I was about to become involved in some of the most heart-wrenching experiences of my life: a fearful trip with my new-found brothers back once again, into the secrets behind the blue door.

TWO STEPS BACK 17

Working with gourds was addictive for me. I always enjoyed transforming simple garden gourds into beautiful representations of ancient pottery, as well as into creative creatures and masks of my own design. The big, annual Wuertz Farm Gourd Show, near Casa Grande, Arizona, had ended, and I was happy for the success I had had selling my artwork there.

I had just returned home from that gourd art show when I got the much-anticipated call that weeks ago, the Crossland Foundation had arranged. I had said *"yes"* to the Foundation's email that had asked whether I would like to correspond with another boy from the ranch. This time the call came from Billy. I was surprised and excited to hear from him after so many years. He was a young boy of about twelve when he was at the boys' ranch. I really liked this kid because he reminded me so much of myself when I was young. He was the kind of boy I would have liked to have had as a son, had I been given a different path to follow in life.

"Hello, Pierre. It's me, William. You know, Billy?"

"Of course, Billy, or should I call you William?"

"No, you can call me Billy."

"I'm so excited that you want to know me again. I have thought of you over the years. I always hoped you would be a survivor and do well in your life." He seemed to hesitate, not knowing how to respond to my comment.

"I live in Tennessee. I've never been married. I drive a semi-truck over and around the country. Not long ago I had a roundtrip drive to Tucson. Guess I passed close to where you live." *How did he know where I live?*

"Wow, that would have been great had I known earlier. We could have met somewhere close by."

"If I do that run again, I want to stop and see you."

"Great Billy. Let's plan on it. Do you remember the time I took you hunting up in the Piney Hills north of the ranch, and we shot that bear?"

"Oh yeah, of course. That was so neat!"

"Well, I have a picture of us with the bear. I'll send it to you."

"OK, Pierre," he said with excitement, "do you remember the rattlesnake we caught?"

"Kind of. We did have a lot of good times together, didn't we?" I told him that I always wished I had had a son like him, and that he was special to me because of that. I was sad that years ago, after he ran away, I was never able to find out where he went.

"That's really nice of you, Pierre, to say that. It means a lot to me, even though I don't think I was that good of a boy back then." I could sense a change in his voice, intimating perhaps thoughts of times at the ranch that were not good for him.

"Billy? Remember that you were just a kid back then. Sometimes when we are young, things can happen to us that are not our fault."

"Pierre" ......followed by a long five seconds of silence, "I drive truck across the states as I told you. When I was going through Texas on my way home from a delivery, I saw a billboard along Interstate 10. It might have been advertising for a hotel, or something like that. One word on the sign stood out for me. It bothered me for days after seeing it."

"What was it, Billy?" I asked with concern.

"It was the word 'Hacienda.' It kind of got in my head, Pierre, and started pulling up memories and feelings, bad things that hurt me. Things that Father Ed did to me. I wrestled with those nightmares all over again. I decided to do something about it. I got up the courage and contacted a law firm in Las Cruces. They are going to take on my case." When I heard the last words he spoke, I could imagine a tornado coming towards both of us, tearing apart our settled lives. But it was up to me at that moment to be supportive and not shrink away from Billy's decision.

"Gee, Billy, this sounds like something you really need to do for yourself."

"I'm to the end of hiding my feelings. All these years of denial, then I saw that sign."

"Well, Billy, I hope I was part of the better times for you to recall. God knows I tried to be there for each of you boys."

"Oh, I know, Pierre. You were the only one that kept me going. The one person that made it bearable. Whenever you would leave on a trip, I would try to run away because you were gone. You were the only one that really cared about me." Those words and the painful thoughts they conveyed fell like a rock to the bottom of my heart. *Oh, dear Jesus! Give us strength.*

"Billy, that's because I loved you and was dedicated to caring for you in an effort to make you happy. Not a possessive love, but one that I've still been giving to you over all these years."

"Thank you so much for that, and all the hikes and hunts, trips to the creek, and those fun night walks too. You were a good teacher and a real big brother to me. So far, Pierre, I have talked several times with the lawyer, and actually met with him. I have something I want to ask you." I could sense my footing giving away on the slippery slope of involvement once again.

"Would it be OK with you if my lawyer could talk to you sometime about things at the ranch and Father Ed?" I had no doubts or hesitations in answering him. My Jesus was with me at that moment, just as strongly as on the first day when I decided years ago to stay and make a commitment to the boys. Yet I hated the thought of having to answer to a lawyer.

"Yes, Billy. That would be fine with me. I don't know what I can add to help, since it has been years, and I may not be able to recall everything, but yes. Count me in. I'll help."

"That's great Pierre. I'll tell Mr. Thomas. He can decide if and when he wants to call you sometime later, OK?"

"You bet, Billy."

"I'm glad we met again, Pierre. I remember so many good times with you. Maybe we can go rattlesnake hunting again. How about that?"

It made me cry inside to think of all the lost years he seemed to want to make up for, as well as the good memories he still hung onto.

"Don't know about them sneaky snakes. How about a walk down the creek, arrowhead hunting instead?"

"Yeah, OK. Let's do that sometime."

We continued to email each other a few more times, but nothing was said again about his lawyer. With that step back towards the past looming in the future, I tried to get back to my normal life, knowing that any day I might have a lawyer knocking at my door.

I know I'm not, as they say, "the sharpest knife in the drawer" when it comes to figuring things out. My past stumbles and trials attest to that. Just the same, though, I tried to do my best for weeks after talking with Billy. About the time when you think you have all your ducks in a row, don't you know a tidal wave is about to hit. The wave came in the form of another bombshell email.

"Hi there, Pierre. I found your name on the internet and want to get to know you again. Here is my number. I hope you will call, Dan."

Was this a coincidence? I began feeling like a yo-yo, and once again God was pulling on the string. That email set me back for some hours while I tried to imagine what was going on. *Why is this happening? First it was Tomás, then Billy and now Dan!* Of course, I was going to call Dan. He was about sixteen years old when I knew him, and he was one of two boys I was to take back East see Niagara Falls on my visit to see my sister in Ohio. Just before that trip, Father Ed refused to let the other boy come with Dan and me. He had to stay with Father. That other boy was Billy.

So, I called. "Hey, Dan. It's me, Pierre. How the heck are you doing?"

"I'm doing just fine. You know it's been so many years, and I wanted to get to know you once again since you were such a good friend to me back then."

"Yeah, a lot of years have gone by. I'm getting pretty old, you know, Dan. Don't climb too many mountains anymore."

"Oh, I know what you mean. Well, Pierre, I'm here in New Mexico. Got a wonderful wife and just got a new grandbaby!"

"Hey, that's great. I can't imagine, you being old too!" I joked, as we both laughed together. What I found in talking to Dan over the next weeks was a seemingly well-adjusted man. I was glad to hear he was doing well after the less encouraging talk with Billy. Dan's life — marriage, raising kids, coping with his job — all spoke of a well-balanced person without deep problems. Eventually, we did talk about troubles at the boys' ranch, but he said he had put it all behind him. Sometime later, I decided to tell him about Billy.

"Hey, Dan, you remember Billy from the ranch? He wrote to me a while back."

"Yes, of course. He used to be one Father Ed picked on a lot."

"Yeah, I know."

"What's Billy been up to?" Feeling that Dan could handle it, I told him.

"Billy is beginning to come to grips with what happened to him at the boys' ranch. He confided in me some of the awful things that Father Ed did to him. Now he is seeking legal help. I guess maybe a lawsuit."

"That's got to be hard on Billy. You suppose he was sexually abused too?" When Dan said that, an alarm went off in my head. Did he mean that Billy was sexually abused as well as being abused in other ways, or did he slip up and mean "as I was abused too"?

Not wanting to question what he said, I quickly answered, "I don't know for sure, Dan, but some years ago, I did some research as a follow-up on Vaughn, the boy who froze to death while running away from the ranch back in 1976. What I found out, I turned over to authorities back then. That material documented a lot of bad things going on behind Father Ed's blue door. I'm so glad that you are OK. Looks like Billy is on a personal journey to heal now."

"Maybe I could call Billy myself, and encourage him," Dan said. "What do you think, Pierre? I'll help him, if he would like me to?"

"For now, Dan, could you wait? I want to first see how things are going for Billy. I haven't heard from him in several weeks. He asked me if I would talk with his lawyer sometime, and I'm still waiting for that call."

"Well, next time you talk to Billy, give him my number and let him know I'll help." Dan seemed so supportive, so solid in his stand for justice, and yet I had a feeling that perhaps he, too, was really troubled deeply inside, unable yet to face his nightmares, the way Billy was now starting to do.

Over time, I thought about these two, now three, boys-grown men, who wrote saying so many nice things about me. I wondered why they thought I was special? All I had tried to do with them were normal, good things. I never thought that was extraordinary the way they seemed to think it was. They seemed to elevate me to a level that made me feel unworthy of such praise. I never wanted such recognition. Just ask Jesus. He knows.

Finally, what I had been waiting for happened. It was the summer of 2014, when the call Billy asked me about came in.

"Hello, is this Pierre L. Nichols?" a man with a low voice asked.

"Yes, it is."

"My name is Dwaine Thomas. I am an attorney representing a client that you know."

SHOW TIME **18**

*U*p until now, I felt that things were progressing at a pace that I could handle. I was happy to be rekindling friendships with the boys from the Hacienda Boys' Ranch. Everything was moving along just fine. I knew that all three now-adult boys from the ranch were communicating with each other; it was good knowing that they were helping each other with their feelings.

Soon enough, the call came from Billy's lawyer, just as he said it would. The attorney, Mr. Dwaine Thomas, was calling from Las Cruces, New Mexico, to set up a meeting with me. At his suggestion, I agreed to the following Friday and offered my home as a meeting place. I could tell he was a smooth talker, telling me how Billy had praised me, thus giving me the impression that he was coming to see how I could help Billy, not to find fault with me. Of course, my mind wouldn't leave the anticipated meeting alone.

During the next week, I busied myself cleaning the house and getting everything set for the meeting. Studio was all cleaned up, coffee ready to start, and a dish of cookies on the table. *Maybe he will stay for a hour or two at the most.* I felt I needed to share some of my previous research with him should he ask, so I dug out the infamous large envelope containing all my boys' ranch papers and notebooks, and had it ready on the kitchen counter should I need it.

All that Thursday night and Friday morning, I began to

worry. *What if someone was trying to pin something on me?* I'm sure Billy would never do anything like that, but a lawyer looking for blood might be different. As I thought about the journey I'd been on, a calm came over me as if my Jesus was again encouraging me, saying, all would be OK, not to worry.

As we had agreed, at 10 A.M., May 16th, 2014, a silvery car pulled into my driveway. Through the side gate came a train of lawyers — not just one, but three of them. They reminded me of funeral directors in black as they carried their sleek leather briefcases. I couldn't help recalling the opening scene in Shakespeare's *Macbeth,* where three devious witches are curling their hands over a fire and delighting in their meeting, saying, "When shall we three meet again?" But they weren't witches. I had to be more positive; there was no turning back. Other than Ms. Billie Surnum, the investigator whom I talked to years ago in Wyoming, I had never had to talk face to face with any lawyers. I began to feel intimidated by their look of authority. *What do they want from me?*

"Good morning to you all," I said. "I'm Pierre." It embarrassed me to realize my nerves were showing as I said that. After proper introductions, we all settled comfortably around the dining room table. I was uncomfortable because all I had to offer these fine professional lawyers was a dish of cookies, but they seemed fine with it and the mugs of coffee.

The senior of the three, Mr. Thomas, was obviously the leader of the pack. Second in command was a pleasant Hispanic man named Steven Hernandez, who took more of a personal interest in me. His comments about the house and my artwork made me feel relaxed. Perhaps that was his role as we sat there making small talk. The third gentleman was obviously the junior member of the team, probably working his way up in the law firm. He seemed rather bored, and rarely spoke at all other than to agree with everything the other two had to say. He looked disdainfully at me when I suggested coffee, so I gave him a bottle of chilled water from the refrigerator.

Mr. Thomas, or "Dwaine" as I was asked to call him since we were all now on a first name basis, did a very satisfying explanation about how Billy had contacted them, wanting to pursue legal recourse against those responsible for messing up his life. All I could say was that I would support Billy however I could. That was the first score for the team of lawyers when I said that.

As the coffee was finished (bottle of water for Junior), I noticed that these smooth-talking lawyers had done their homework. Oh, they were clever and professional as they asked me questions! I was a player in a well-rehearsed skit which they had all planned out ahead of time. They shared some of the details of what Billy had told them, but they were here not to tell his story, but to listen to mine. More specifically, they wanted my records. They were somehow aware of my research and documents, perhaps from the Crossland Foundation, or even from the documents from Billie Surnum's case years ago. Finally, Dwaine asked whether I had any papers or documentation that might show how the archbishop of Santa Fe handled the situation concerning Father Ed at the boys' ranch.

Of course, I had material that could be crucial for the case against the archdiocese of Santa Fe. It was decision time for me.

Should I give it over to them or not? Which way Jesus, for the protection of the archdiocese, or the well-being of Billy?

I stood up and my body seemed to float over to the kitchen counter. The envelope full of pain and tears felt extra heavy when I picked it up. Turning around, I walked that half mile back to the table where the lawyers were silently sitting. Once I took my seat, I laid my arms across the bulging envelope on the table, lowered my head, and said a silent prayer as they waited in anticipation for my next move. I needed to know that my Jesus was with me. I also wanted them to know that handing over all my information was a deeply emotional experience for me. After a minute, I raised my head and calmly said, "This is what you came for, I know." I was no longer nervous. I sensed a calm come over me and I heard those haunting words, "Just let go."

"Yes, Pierre, it is true." Dwaine said to me. I could see sincerity in his eyes for the first time. It made me feel good to be able to help out. I sensed that what I had in that envelope before them would be crucial in supporting Billy's case against the Archdiocese of Santa Fe.

When I opened the envelope and poured out the contents of diaries, notes and stacks of papers, I could see it was they who were nervous. They couldn't hide their excitement. It was like giving meat to a hungry dog. When I showed them the copies of the letters to Archbishop Sanchez, it was as if they had just won the lottery. I caught them flashing glances at each other as if to say, "*We got them!*" It made me kind of chuckle to myself thinking, *they're nothing in their fancy suits and smooth talk, nothing without my documents!* I could have been clever and asked, "How much is it worth to you?" but I remembered Billy.

His well-being and healing would be compensation enough. The lawyers tried to cover their excitement as they reviewed all my material. From time to time they would ask a question about a detail. I freely answered them all, no longer caring about keeping anything from them, but it did make me feel used.

"Pierre, because of the extent of your material, would you allow us to take it with us so we can correlate it and be able to better present your facts to help poor Billy?" Dwaine asked. I didn't miss the implication of implied quilt had I said no. "If this material will be used to help Billy, you may take it with you to copy on the condition that it all will remain as my personal property AND be returned to me intact later in the year." They all agreed.

The end of the meeting came some three to four hours later that day. It had been exhausting. I had come to almost like the three lawyers. I had to. They had my material in their hands and they had Billy too! I had to trust them. Dwaine carefully packed all my material into their three briefcases, and we said goodbye before they headed back to Las Cruces.

I closed the front door, and sat down again at the table to munch on the cookies, trying to clear my mind. It dawned on me that eating all the cookies wasn't going to fill the empty feeling I had inside. I felt empty having nothing more I could do. I was in control of nothing, with no cards left in my hand to play. They were in control of the future. Not an easy feeling, being left in the hands of lawyers.

Meanwhile, it was good to know that Billy, Tomás and Dan were now emailing one other about their personal experiences. As the weeks passed by, I heard little about any legal proceedings. A month or two later in 2014, I called Mr. Thomas in Las Cruces to ask what was happening. He seemed rather impersonal and tight-lipped about saying anything to me. He did say, though, that his law firm was now representing all three men, not only Billy. That was a welcome surprise to me. I guess the three found strength among themselves to get together and face the trauma that would ensue from a legal showdown with the archdiocese of Santa Fe. I was glad for that, but I couldn't help feeling that I was no longer a partner in what was happening. I didn't want to ask the boys-men about what they went through at the hands of Father Ed at the boys' ranch, and I knew the lawyers weren't about to tell me anything either.

I felt bad about being outside the loop, not because the boys weren't saying anything to me, since they were probably told not to, but because the lawyers didn't share what was going on. I thought they could have been a little more considerate knowing how much I cared about what was happening.

Finally, I did get a call from Las Cruces. It was Mr. Thomas, saying that depositions were being taken in Albuquerque. They needed me to go and give mine. I realized the seriousness of it, understanding that I would have to tell everything I knew in response to the questions that were going to be asked of me. Hoping for an excuse to avoid this experience, I said that I had no funds to make such a trip; but they assured me my costs would be covered. A week later, I packed my best clothes and drove to the designated hotel in Albuquerque where the three lawyers would be waiting for me.

I had never stayed in such a swanky hotel before. I rode

in a glass-sided elevator up to the fourth floor while I looked down at the open lobby area. My room was a large fancy suite. I was being treated like royalty. *Maybe this was part of my last meal before having to face the firing squad.* When I returned to the lobby, I met Mr. Thomas, Mr. Hernandez and Junior. The atmosphere was much more informal than the first time we met. Mr. Thomas was without a suit coat, Mr. Hernandez was also in casual clothes; however, Junior was still in his suit, of course.

The conversation in the lobby was among the three of them arguing over which fancy restaurant we should all go to for dinner. I thought it was a show to impress me — three roosters trying to out-crow each other. Once they agreed on where we were going to eat, a hotel limousine drove us to an exclusive restaurant where we gathered around our private table. I was beginning to feel self-conscious, hoping I wouldn't look ignorant when the time would come for me to pick from the menu. While the three of them were discussing which drinks were their favorites, I was trying to figure out how to pronounce Cabernet Sauvignon. The menu was impressive. I noticed that there were no prices on it. After the three of them settled on ordering steaks, I decided to do the same thing. When the steaks came, they were gigantic!

Dinner continued as they talked among themselves. They seemed to revel in telling their stories of when they each made their first million. I thought to myself, *Yeah, with my proof of the archdiocese's responsibility, with my documentation, and with all three boys as their sacrificial lambs, I'm sure they were planning their next millions already!* But I acted gracious, smiling and trying to look interested in all they were joking about.

I noticed how little they were eating — several bites from

the steak and it was pushed aside. Special side dishes that they had ordered were never touched beyond a spoonful or were completely ignored. I felt disgusted. I couldn't help thinking about the street people of Los Angeles, and who might be out at the back of the restaurant here, waiting at the dumpster, hungry and thankful for their waste. I couldn't follow their example. I made sure I ate everything on my plate and drank all three glasses of the fancy wine they kept offering me. Could I have asked for a to-go box? Probably that would have embarrassed them. No, I didn't, so I let them embarrass me with their wastefulness.

I was glad when it was over and we were back at the hotel. Something was wrong with the building, though. It wobbled and swayed all the way up to the fourth floor. Once in my room, I slumped across the king bed, thinking about myself while my head was spinning around. I saw my life turning into a joke, a life of being fooled by my trust in others. *I'm such a loser!* All I could do now was follow through with tomorrow's deposition . . . *whatever that is.* My final act. I think I wept for myself, self-pity brought on by the wine. *So what! Go to sleep, Pierre, you're drunk.*

My alarm sounded early the next morning. I had time to screw my head back on and go to the lobby for some breakfast. The inner lobby of the hotel was like the hollow middle of a big cruise ship. All the rooms surrounded the lobby, every floor looking down. In the lobby people were busy visiting and milling around the extensive array of steam tables that offered every kind of breakfast food you could think of.

I took the glass elevator down to the lobby and back up to the top floor to enjoy the experience, hoping no one noticed my silliness. Once back down to the lobby, I proceeded to get something to eat. I felt relaxed, *no one here knows of my troubles.* It made me feel good being among smiling, happy-looking people. A man sitting over at one of the plush couches looked relaxed as he reviewed a newspaper. I wished at that moment I could have felt as relaxed as he did; it was going to be a stressful morning for me. I was finishing up my last bit of bacon when I saw the three lawyers coming toward me from the elevator.

"Good morning, Pierre." Mr. Thomas said. "I trust you slept well last night?" The three of them smirked knowingly at me, indicating they knew the wine had done its work.

"Oh yeah," I joked back. "just hope I didn't sign anything!" That was our last laugh together that day. All the comradery of last night, the joking and kidding around, were gone now. They were back to suitcoats and had no desire for coffee or small talk. It was time to go downtown for the deposition. We took the elevator to our rooms to freshen up, to go to the bathroom, and for me at least, to say one more private prayer.

The limousine was at the entrance waiting for us. I had a feeling of panic, wanting to run away and not get into that car. *Couldn't they do this without me?* I pleaded to my Jesus. He reminded me of my boys and my commitment. We all got into the limo and away we went.

Thoughts spun in my head as I tried to organize them before I had to face the meeting. I remembered some of the details that I had learned from talking with Mr. Thomas, details of how the depositions had gone with the three boys. He told me how painful it was for one of the boys to have to admit that the times he was abused numbered in the hundreds; how poor Dan, who

I thought was so well adjusted, broke down on the floor crying while telling of his abuse. It made my heart fill with sadness. All those things which I had learned I was now instructed to put aside, and let my own deposition proceed by telling my side of the sad story.

"When you are asked a question, Pierre, answer honestly in as few words as you can. Do not add anything else," Mr. Thomas advised me. He seemed concerned that I might say too much and get trapped by my own words. I began to get apprehensive thinking that maybe the lawyers for the archdiocese of Santa Fe might be out to trip me up. I intended to answer them respectfully, but also with enough of an answer to satisfy myself, although not necessarily satisfy Mr. Thomas. If this was going to be my chance to help clarify issues in defense of the boys, that was what I wanted to do. I had nothing to hide and I had Jesus on my side.

The car pulled up at the curb of the office building on Third Street, downtown Albuquerque. With nothing more to say, we silently proceeded up the elevator to the Bernalillo Second District Offices. The plain white walls were occasionally accented with framed paintings. It could have been any hall in any hospital or business. A door opened on the left, and we were welcomed to take our seats along the far side of a large rectangular conference table.

The room was brightly lit, and there were bottles of water on the table. That told me that the meeting might last more than an hour. Minutes later, after final reassuring smiles from Mr. Thomas and Mr. Hernandez, the door opened. In walked three men in suits, followed by a court reporter who quickly took her seat, ready to record every word of the proceedings. The senior gentleman who was representing the Archdiocese of Santa Fe extended his hand across the table to greet me. I was impressed by his warmth and friendliness, considering the circumstances. With everyone in place the meeting started. JOHN DOE 36 vs. ARCHDIOCESE OF SANTA FE. July 16, 2014, Monday, 9:11 A.M.

I looked nervously at the center of the big table. There, sitting like a time bomb waiting to go off, was my stuffed manila envelope with all my papers and documentation that Mr. Thomas had brought with him. The meeting began with formal introductions, after which I was sworn in. All the evidence from my envelope had to be meticulously recorded. Each item, such as photos from the boys' ranch, staff notes, letters between me and Father Ed, as well as the all-important copies of letters to Archbishop Sanchez, all had to be confirmed by me and given an exhibit number. It was a slow process which resulted in over fifty-five exhibits. With that finally finished, the questioning began.

By now I was feeling comfortable about facing the archdiocesan lawyers. They were courteous and patient with me as I answered each question. There was so much emphasis on my verifying information that I'm sure at least an hour passed before we got into questions about the Hacienda, Father Ed and the boys. All the while, Mr. Thomas sat back, glancing at me with the look of a fisherman watching the bobber, should he need to pull it in to check his bait. I was wordy at times, but I was determined to let the archdiocesan lawyers know all the details, that went along with simple answers. I was relaxed, and I could sense that they were not judging me nor trying to trick me. The questioning was extremely detailed.

Q. "Tell me what the washroom (at the boys' ranch) is."

Q. "How many toilets, sinks, where did Father Ed shower?"

Q. "Tell me about the double doors in the hall to the boys' room."

Q. "Tell me about the Sisters."

Q. "Tell me about Exhibit #34, then # 44," and so on.

It took me hours to explain each detail and to answer the hundreds of questions, but I didn't mind. I figured that those lawyers had already heard the boys' depositions, and that the outcome of this case was already determined. What I could add was confirmation of the things they had heard earlier.

There were a few times when I could not remember what I had said years ago; sometimes I felt angry and let everyone hear it. When the time came for me to recall how I stood up in front of Archbishop Sanchez and pointed my finger at him, I also did the same thing to the archdiocesan lawyers. Mr. Thomas quickly suggested we take a short break, probably wanting to "reel me in," to give me a chance to calm down so he could advise me. But I was quick to say that I would rather continue. I knew Mr. Thomas wasn't pleased, but I was on a roll and didn't want to stop.

So many minute details, and all of them brought back images and memories as I tried my best to answer the questions. When I had to tell about Vaughn's running away I could not hold back my tears. I could see even in the eyes of the archdiocesan lawyers a shared sorrow, one that let me know that what I was testifying to would be useful in settling the case in favor of the boys. It was a tiring and exhausting session.

Finally, in the afternoon, an archdiocesan lawyer asked his last question. Then he simply said, "All right. Thank you. Nothing further." Mr. Thomas asked me a few questions, and after a short while he also said, "I have no further questions. Thank you." Asked if I wanted a copy of my deposition, I said, "Yes."

With that the meeting was officially over. It was now 4:34 P.M., seven hours and forty-eight minutes, and 256 pages of my testimony, later. As we were all about to leave the conference table, I had one last thought that I wanted to share with the archdiocesan lawyers. I leaned over the table and raising my finger toward them one last time, I said what perhaps I should have said earlier.

"You have no idea what effect Father Ed and the Hacienda have had on MY life!"

RETURN OF THE RAVENS 19

I t was good to be home in Silver City after that stressful ordeal in Albuquerque. Even though I believed I had done my best in answering all the questions the lawyers had asked, I still questioned myself. *Had I done enough? Would Tomás, Billy and Dan be proud of me?* Would Vaughn above all be proud of me? All this turmoil had its beginning with him. Every success for the boys in the lawsuit would be a win for Vaughn. If the boys were taken care of, I imagined Vaughn would be pleased.

After all the trauma of that week, I felt rather lost, wandering around at home, hoping to hear something about the outcome of the lawsuit. The following week, to my surprise and delight, I got a phone call from Dan. He was excited as he shouted into the phone, "Hey, Pierre, we won! We won our case! We are all here in Albuquerque, talking about it and sharing pictures and everything. They thought they could get by with only awarding settlements to two of us, but we insisted. All three get equal settlements, or none of us. They reconsidered, and we won. We're celebrating!"

"Wow, Dan, that's great." I said, "I'm happy for all of you, and really proud you all spoke up for one other. No more secrets from behind that blue door, not anymore."

"That's right, Pierre. Tomás and Billy also want to say thanks to you too. Without you, we might not have won." Sensing the end of a long journey, I was full of emotion as I said, "I love you all." I wanted to ask Dan about how they were coping, as well as about details of the settlement. Would they receive some kind of financial settlement? More importantly, would they receive professional counselling to help them move forward in their lives. But it was a celebration call from Dan, a call that told me all I really needed to know. What the three men had said, or what the lawyers agreed on, wasn't important to me. I was satisfied. Weeks after that, I received this letter from Mr. Thomas, on behalf of the law firm in Las Cruces:

Pierre:

I want you to know that Billy, Tomas and Dan's cases all settled at a mediation in Albuquerque last month. I want to thank you for all of the input and knowledge and help which you provided over the past two years. Your contributions were essential to pushing the Archdiocese to settle these cases for sums which, according to their own estimation, are higher than they've paid in any of their other hundreds of cases of priest abuse. I also want you to know how important your contributions were personally to Billy, Tomas and Dan. You were, as they all said, their only safe harbor as children at the Hacienda, and you were again ready and willing to help so many decades later in this litigation. All three, will receive funds sufficient to allow them to finally move forward with their lives.

Dwaine Thomas

It was a good letter to receive, but it left me still wishing that he would have let me know of the settlement day, so I too could have been there, celebrating. It would probably have been the only chance I would ever have to meet all three men, together, face to face. But years ago, I had learned something: part of love is letting go — letting them move on with their lives, and, if necessary, without me. The three boys-men would be taken care of, and I was happy to see the end of their quest for justice.

But my journey was to take another unexpected turn, bringing about a wonderful conclusion. Dr. Podles of the Crossland Foundation, the organization that investigates pedophilia cases within the Catholic Church, received an email which he forwarded to me. The email was from a woman named Eldora. She was one of the young sisters of Vaughn, and she was now in her forties. She had started reading his book, *Sacrilege,* about sexual abuse in the church, but couldn't stomach reading it through. She asked Dr. Podles questions she had about her brothers, Vaughn and Alan. She also asked if he could help her locate where Vaughn was buried. He wrote to me knowing that I, more than anyone else, would be able to help her. I felt it would be an honor to help, so I sent an email to her up near Farmington, New Mexico. I told her about the boys' ranch and even about some of the troubling times we all had had there, both as staff and boys, under the control of Father Ed.

I think I overwhelmed her at first with all I had to share with her. That was the first of several tearful conversations we had over the following weeks. I was able to tell her about both Alan and Vaughn, and how they loved hiking and exploring the outdoors. I wanted Eldora to know that they were both normal, good kids.

"Did my brothers ever get abused, Pierre?" Eldora asked. I knew that question would come up eventually, so I tried to be prepared for the answer I would have to give her.

"Some things are hard to know when they are hidden from view, or covered over in shame." I replied. "I now know that many of the boys at the ranch unfortunately were abused. I cannot say for sure whether your brothers were among those boys. What I do know is, that Vaughn and the other boy he was with ran away because they didn't want to do what Father Ed wanted them to do with him. It was an honorable decision that caused them to face the weather on that cold fateful night." I could tell she was weeping as I gave her that answer.

"But what about Alan?" she asked. "He felt bad because he didn't go with his brother that night. He never talked about anything from the boys' ranch. It had to be part of the reason for his unhappiness, getting involved in drugs and breaking the law."

"Well, Eldora, all we can do now is think of your brothers with compassion and love. For the short time I knew them, I believe they were normal boys, hoping and coping the best they could at that time."

These conversations with Vaughn's sister were, no doubt, hard on her. After so many years of wondering and wanting to know more, now she was coping with the full story. I was trying my best to help ease the pain. Of course, the initial question had been, whether I could help her find Vaughn's grave. She was young when her brother Vaughn died, and their mother didn't keep any record for her other children of the location of the cemetery. Eldora was excited when I told her where it was.

"Will I be able to find it?" she asked.

I told her how to drive out from Raton, where the turn was down the gravel road, and where to watch for the little white church of Our Lady of Mount Carmel. "When you go to the back of the cemetery, there you will find Vaughn's grave close to the juniper trees."

"But how will I know it's his grave?" she asked with concern.

"Eldora, you will know." I replied. "There is a nice granite headstone there at his grave."

"But who would have done that? Who would have done such a nice thing?" In the flash of a second, I seemed to be transported to a place of pure light, and I could see my Jesus smiling at me, giving me a moment of joy for what I had done for both Vaughn and Eldora. Holding back my emotions as best I could, I said, "Dear Eldora, I put the stone on his grave years ago. I wanted Vaughn to be honored and remembered."

It took her a moment to reply. When she could talk again, she said, "You are Vaughn's angel, Pierre. How wonderful and loving you truly are." I was moved, hearing how happy she was. I suggested that since they now knew where Vaughn's grave was, sometime maybe Alan would like to go there and see for himself where his brother is buried.

After that last call, I knew my journey for Vaughn was coming to an end, but the real gift came in a phone call from Eldora a month later. Addressing me as "my dear Pierre," she said, "I will forever be grateful to you for your love and commitment to my brothers. All these years of wondering where Vaughn was and now I know. My heart is full of love and happiness since recently I have been to Vaughn's grave. With the help of my daughter, we made the trip to the cemetery last week. We saw the beautiful stone you so caringly put on Vaughn's grave.

I can't thank you enough, other than to send you my love and gratitude."

With a change in her voice, she said, "There is something you didn't know, that I share very personally and tearfully with you, Pierre." I could hear her sigh before she continued.

"When Alan came home with us years ago, after Vaughn's funeral, Mother was worried about him. Alan would not talk to her about anything from the boys' ranch. He would go outside our little house, hiding for hours at a time. Then it was drugs and getting in trouble with the law. He was never a happy boy.

"When we went to the cemetery last week, my daughter parked the SUV along the side of that country road. Opening the wire gate to the pasture, we walked through the grass up to the little white church. With heavy heart, we made our way through the graveyard as I recalled my sad childhood memories. At the back near the junipers, like you said, we found Vaughn's grave. It was a special moment given to me by you, Pierre. The gravestone gave me a feeling of peace. A feeling, like family, we were all finally together again. You see, Pierre," she explained crying over the phone, "three years ago, Alan died from a drug overdose, in 2011. I laid his ashes on Vaughn's grave so they would finally be together again."

What a painful, yet satisfying feeling Eldora must have had that day at Vaughn's grave, bringing Alan there to be with his brother. My hopes for her were that she could lay to rest her worries, and finally move on with her life, just as I was hoping I could do. I felt very close to her, having shared part of our journeys together.

Days later after we had talked, I was thinking about Dan,

Tomás and Billy, and the long journey Jesus took me on for Vaughn's sake. It was then that I felt a sense of peace come over me. A sense of *fin,* as my *ma mère* would say. I found myself back there at Vaughn's grave one last time. Everything was fresh and green as the warm sun shone down from a clear blue sky. I could see the ravens silently circling high above the junipers, looking down with joy. It gave me cause to recall again those reoccurring words spoken to me so many years ago, those words of peace that I lovingly shared with Eldora. Finally, I too could,

"Just let go."

EPILOGUE

BEYOND THE DOOR

Since 2014, I have continued to live in New Mexico. Writing *Secrets of the Blue Door* was a very personal and painful experience; however, I was able to finish this, thanks to my faith and to my longtime friend, Jesus. I felt his presence in all I did back then, even though my naiveté and weakness were obstacles along my journey to find justice. In spite of this, I believe the best did come from the mission I was destined to carry out.

In writing this memoir I wanted, among other things, to achieve a sense of closure for myself. I also wanted to share my journey so that others will know that working with youth requires everyone to look carefully and act quickly should we find someone abusing children.

I have learned that Archbishop Robert Sanchez was removed from his position as archbishop by Pope John Paul II in 1993, due to a scandal in which Sanchez had been involved with numerous women during his time as archbishop. He spent his last years in seclusion and died in 2012.

Father Edward Francis Donelan, after years of being moved from parish to parish without being held accountable for his actions, was given a respectable retirement by Archbishop Sheehan in 1994, and finally passed away later that year, never having to answer for the abuse he caused or to anyone's law, at least not here on earth.

Some parts of my story are a matter of public record. Some

of the names have been changed to protect privacy. Except for Vaughn, I changed the names of all the boys mentioned in my memoir who were connected to the Hacienda de los Muchachos Boys Ranch. Names of adults are accurate, though most of the people involved have since passed away.

I will always feel sad for the damage Father Ed did to the boys under his care, as well as for the negligence of the Catholic Church and its cover-up of sexual abuse. Vaughn was the first of several boys who have died in the years since the Hacienda de los Muchachos Boys Ranch. Mental problems, addictions, poor health, even car accidents, have claimed their share of my family of brothers.

As I look forward to what years I have left, I am happy to continue with the friendships I have with survivors of the Hacienda. Billy, Dan and Tomás gained justice for themselves, for Vaughn, and maybe for others who had suffered at the hands of a pedophile.

Many happy chapters in my life were omitted from my memoir. I left out many meaningful pages to focus on this important story I wanted to share. It is a story that I hope conveys how courage and endurance can conquer wrong, how everyone must be vigilant, standing up against child abuse, to expose any wolf in sheep's clothing, regardless of his position or authority.

As I enjoy my retirement years, I am blessed each day with faith, friends and love. When the sun comes to set on my last day on earth, I hope, *stay with me Jesus!* to see my ravens flying with angels, accompanying me to a restful place, knowing I tried to do my best through all the journeys of my life.

Pierre L. Nichols

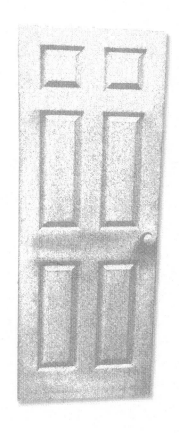

ABOUT THE AUTHOR

Pierre L. Nichols, grew up in Chicago and Oak Park, Illinois. After his high school years, and a scholarship to the Chicago Art Institute, he joined the army serving overseas in Thailand as an army photographer. After service in the military, he was employed as a commercial photographer in Youngstown, Ohio, until an invite to be a volunteer in New Mexico changed his life. It was while working as a volunteer at a boys' ranch for troubled youth, that Nichols discovered sexual abuse by the ranch founder. Investigations by him, produced little results from any authorities. After so much heartbreak and sadness over the tragic death of one boy, as well as his own personal struggles with faith, Nichols moved on with his life. He did work with migrant workers, street people and developed a successful art gallery in Wyoming, before returning to New Mexico in 2004. It was then that the boys ranch issue resurfaced, forty years later. Nichols goes through the pain and anguish all over again, to help bring justice for the boys that were so harmed, as well as closure for himself. Nichols lives a full life as an artist and writer in Silver City, New Mexico.

Made in the USA
San Bernardino, CA
15 February 2018